MY SAND LIFE,
MY PEBBLE LIFE

MY SAND LIFE, MY PEBBLE LIFE

A memoir of a childhood and the sea

ADLARD COLES

LONDON • OXFORD • NEW YORK • NEW DELHI • SYDNEY

ADLARD COLES
Bloomsbury Publishing Plc
50 Bedford Square, London, WC1B 3DP, UK
29 Earlsfort Terrace, Dublin 2, Ireland

BLOOMSBURY, ADLARD COLES and the Adlard Coles logo are trademarks of
Bloomsbury Publishing Plc

First published in Great Britain 2022

A catalogue record for this book is available from the British Library

Library of Congress Cataloguing-in-Publication data has been applied for

ISBN: HB: 978-1-4729-8294-0; ePub: 978-1-4729-8295-7; ePDF 978-1-4729-8296-4

2 4 6 8 10 9 7 5 3 1

Typeset by Deanta Global Publishing Services, Chennai, India
Printed and bound in Great Britain by CPI Group (UK) Ltd, Croydon, CR0 4YY

To find out more about our authors and books visit www.bloomsbury.com and sign up for
our newsletters

Contents

Introduction: COASTING

I very rarely make plans for my writing; I admire thriller writers who paper the wall with Post-it notes and science fantasy authors who make spreadsheets and histories for the worlds they're creating. Even when I'm writing something that should be planned, like a radio play, I just crack a cup of tea over the vessel of my ideas (it's too early in the morning for champagne) and set sail on an uncharted voyage. This has meant that the producers and directors have had to work very hard with me to help me to produce something that has plot and character rather than images and gags and so with this new book I decided I'd learned my lesson and I would make a plan. Maybe I wouldn't go as far as spreadsheets, but I would certainly have a compass. A metaphorical compass, of course, but it would be a start.

The idea of the book was that I would write about the coast of Britain; sometimes I would delve into my memories of places I'd visited, and sometimes I would visit new places and write about what I encountered. I would try and knit connections between the two and, like all writers unless they're liars, I would imagine the author photograph of a windswept me gazing out at the eternal water, perhaps with an ironic ice cream in my hand.

My plan for the book was based around my quest to do a gig in every village hall in the country with my musician mate Luke Carver Goss. If the coast was within striking distance, by which I mean of a railway because I can't drive, of the village hall we'd played the night before, I would go there the next day and absorb it on the (metaphorical again) blotting paper I wrote on. This may not seem like much of a plan if you're a thriller writer on the fourteenth book of a series featuring a hard-bitten detective with a complex home life and a passion for vintage china but let me tell you that for me it's a plan.

And then the pandemic's tide started to come in. In early March 2020 my wife and I had a couple of days in Scarborough, the jewel of the East Coast; the plan was that this would make the first chapter of the book. Except that things felt a little chilly, and that wasn't just the wind blowing across the sand. We went into shops to try to buy hand sanitiser but there was none. People looked nervous; there seemed to be a sense of hurry about them as though they wanted to rush somewhere but, crucially, they weren't quite sure where. In our Premier Inn there was no buffet breakfast and we were served by a waiter who said 'This is how it will be for a little while' and I felt a deep sadness, partly because of his turn of phrase and partly because I couldn't get seven sausages, a croissant and a tub of Greek yoghurt. After all, like everybody else in the Western world, I'd become used to treating life as a buffet that endlessly invited me to graze. My wife and I felt a desire to sit far away from strangers and closer to each other. Walking towards the castle, we wondered aloud to each other whether we should have come. The strong wind made me weep. I think it was the strong wind.

And then, about a week after we came back home and I shook the sand out of my notebook, the country locked down and all my gigs fell off a cliff and my diary relaxed in its emptiness and lack of scribblings. The village halls of Britain were safe from my laboured gags. My children and grandchildren could no longer visit the house and we had to make do with drive-by wavings and Zoom quizzes that nobody really wanted to win. I still wanted to write this book, so I had to have a new plan, and the new plan was to use the time to climb deeper into my memories of the coast, of the places I'd been and the person I was when I went there. Two slices of the coast would loom large: Cleethorpes, where my wife's family have had a caravan for decades, and where my 92-year-old mother-in-law would happily spend all summer, until 2020 put a lock on all that and forced her into a foreshortened season where she daren't go on a bus; and Northumberland, where my children have had wonderful times and where my wife and I have discovered solace and calm over the years.

Brief unlockings like the one in the summer of that year allowed us out and it meant the sea air in the sentences was fresh rather than air-conditioned by memory, but mostly I paddled in the half-remembered and, I admit, half-invented past. And so the coast became a place of legend and myth; its unchanging narrative of tides and whirling gulls shape-shifted into my own story, a story of someone who, in their mid-sixties, was being nudged into a state of endless reverie by the lockdowns and the pandemic. I found that because I wore my mask a lot, I couldn't wear my glasses as much as I usually did; the mask and my breathing steamed them up. I went to the optician's and she said that my eyes were improving; I asked how that could be possible, given my advancing age. 'It sometimes happens,' she said in the half-darkness. I didn't question further but I reckoned it was because the turbulent times had turned my gaze inward, towards an internal and personal coastline.

So, if you're expecting a guidebook, look away now. If you want a map, I suggest that you make your own because I think you'll know your roads much better than I do. Welcome to my coast; come with me and wander its paths. You might not find your way back home; I'm not sure if I ever will.

BAREFOOT IN THE SAND IN BLACKPOOL

I was fifteen years old and I was planning a trip to Blackpool with my mates Bards and Smalesy; we were an inseparable trio whose nights out mainly consisted of wandering around the mining village where we lived and ending up at the fish shop for some chips with bits on. The pit bus would pass like an image of a world that would never change because this was the 1970s and there were certainties scattered between the loud revolutions and thinking that excited our young and impressionable minds.

In a complex domestic arrangement, Bards lived with his grandma near Barnsley and his parents lived in Blackpool; this was so that Bards could finish his schooling and not have his education disrupted, which made sense to us all as an idea because living with your grandma felt like fun and she certainly didn't mind him being out eating chips on a school night.

One Monday evening he announced that his parents had invited us to stay in Blackpool for a few days and that his dad would come and pick us up and take us after school on the coming Friday. I was suddenly overcome with an emotional and romantic idea: 'I'll tell you what, lads,' I said (imagine my voice still breaking, still tinkling like glass, still warbling like a harmonica under water), 'let's stay up all night and walk to the beach to see the sunrise.' They nodded and then Smalesy said,

'And let's do it in bare feet.' Ah, the early 1970s: history's tie-dyed bucket, half full of hope.

At Maison Bards, we decided to do the all-night adventure on our third night; the first night was spent hunting for decent chips and avoiding gulls. Of course the chips were excellent because we were by the sea but of course we said they were inferior because we were teenagers from Yorkshire. The second night we thought we'd just stay in watching *Dr Who* on TV because, yes, we were teenagers from Yorkshire. On the fourth night we'd got tickets to see the hippy musical *Hair* at the theatre; it seemed that Bards had convinced his parents it was a family saga about barbers, which was fine by us because we were looking forward very much indeed to the nudity. It was the Age of Aquarius, you know; we could pretend we were seeing the show and the sunrise in California.

Bards's parents were fine about us wandering down to the beach on our own in the early hours, although his dad did say, 'If any coppers stop you, tell them you're looking for Ripley's Believe It or Not!' We nodded sagely. I was a big fan of Ripley's Believe It or Not! in the American comics I bought. We decided to leave the house on our sunrise pilgrimage at 4am, something that we thought would feel like a moment in a beat poet's diary. We never thought to check what time the sun actually rose, of course. That kind of detail never occurred to us.

We all found staying up late a bit of a strain. We took turns at guessing what time it was and we were crushingly disappointed when it was 11.48pm not 2am but eventually 4am arrived as though it was on the last carriage of a slow train and we set off through half-dark streets to the sea. Our excitement was volcanic and epic, no doubt stoked up by our lack of sleep. We were going to commune with the sand and the water. Our bare feet would snog the waves and the feeling would be so exquisite that we wouldn't be able to tell The Other Lads about it when we got back home but we'd try, oh yes we'd try.

We took our shoes off when we left the house and carried them along like talismen. I remember, all these years later, that it was unpleasant. The pavement was rough and sometimes sharp and there were meandering archipelagos of dog detritus to tack past. The sea called to us; or was it the shout of a man who had lost the name of his B&B somewhere in the back of his brain's wardrobe?

My feet really hurt but the sky was experiencing a pre-sunrise lightening. We got closer and closer to the nirvana of the beach. A police car slowed and stopped and a copper wound a window down and stuck his head out. He looked like Fancy Smith in *Z Cars*. 'Lost your shoes, boys?' he asked nonchalantly. We held our shoes up and he nodded. 'Where are you off to?' he asked. There was no urgency in his voice but I was scared. A gull laughed uproariously. 'We're going to Ripley's Believe It or Not!,' I squeaked, dropping one of my shoes. 'I believe you,' he said, either winking or blinking.

Ripley's Believe It or Not!, now just called Ripley's like a nightclub in Derbyshire, is a place where you can experience oddities and cracks in the universe; originally based on a strip that appeared in American newspapers, it's now a franchise of books, magazines and museums like the one in Blackpool. If you want to see shrunken heads or find out whether turkeys can blush or not, then Ripley's is for you. Outside Ripley's Believe It or Not! in those days there was a tap that appeared to be suspended in mid-air but from which, amazingly, *water appeared to gush.* (My italics.) I'd seen this on TV and was eager to witness it at first hand, like a Druid would be very keen to catch a glimpse of Stonehenge. We walked, our feet getting increasingly ragged, towards the tap. It was, in my memory, about 5am. The sun was not yet up but the sky was smouldering a little. The tap wasn't turned on. We gazed at it and we spotted a clear Perspex tube going from the tip of the tap to the floor. So that was it; so that was the trick or, being charitable, the clever device.

My soul felt like my feet; scraped and grazed. A little shard of innocence fell away. Then a minor miracle happened: the tap was turned on by something automatic in the depths of the building and the water splashed and we could believe again that we couldn't believe it. We turned towards the sea. 'Have they really got nowt on in that *Hair*?' said Bards, using the word 'that' in the Barnsley way. We assured him that it was true, tuppence and all. We walked towards the sea. We felt the balm of the sand between our mucky adolescent toes. We gazed at the sky. We thought there was something wrong with the sun; it was refusing to rise even though the sky was clear and it was getting quite light. Yes, you're right. The sun rises in the East and Blackpool is in the West. We were halfway through the first act of *Hair* gazing at a naked bottom when we realised that.

ONE DAY THAT BOY WILL BE PRIME MINISTER

My earliest memory of the coast may not be a memory at all; it may be a fiction, or a false recollection, or a photograph that maybe I glimpsed in a long-lost album and maybe I didn't. It could be something that I partly imagined and partly lived through but I'll write it down as though it's a bundle of facts and a few officially licensed poetic images and we'll see how close that gets us to the water lapping at the shore.

It's true that my dad was in the Royal Navy from 1937 until 1958, and he spent the last few months of his career in Plymouth waiting to go home and start a new life that didn't involve the floor moving under him. And it's true that I was born in 1956. It's true that Darfield, the village I've always lived in near Barnsley, had a station until Beeching redacted it and so it's possible, just possible, that I might have got the train down to Plymouth with my mother to visit my dad and we might have stayed in a hotel near the sea and we might have gone for a walk on the Hoe. I was told this so often and I've told it to myself so often that, even if it isn't true, it's McMillan True, or Plymouth True, or Poetically True, and they're better than boring old True. One other fact: my dad had the sea in his blood, and I don't, and I've often tried to fathom these differences in my thinking and my writing. Without getting too close to the waves.

Here's what 'happened': My mother is running from our house to Darfield station and somehow she is carrying me because it's 1958 and I'm too young to run all the way from Barnsley Road. The platform is wreathed in steam like the platforms in *Brief Encounter*, a film I know my mother was a big fan of although I wouldn't have known that at the time. I remember, or 'recall', a train door slamming and there was rain on the train windows. We must have changed trains at least a couple of times but those moments have sunk into the sponge and all I can see behind my mind's glasses is the rain on that window. I think I remember my mother smoking.

Then suddenly we're in Plymouth and there are gulls; I vividly remember the gulls, the same gulls that are the soundtrack to this book. Or perhaps just the one gull like The Ancient Mariner's albatross, hanging round my ample neck as I tell this tale. We are walking (I'm being pushed in a big Silver Cross pram, surely?) by the sea and my dad is wearing his uniform and he's pointing at a big ship, which I now know is the aircraft carrier the HMS *Ark Royal* but which at the time seemed to be a piece of metal as big as the shout of the gulls in my little ears.

The sea is vast and it converses with itself and its waving waves. We go right up to the ship and it is like standing next to a skyscraper or a cliff face. Suddenly in my memory or my dream or my fiction we are on the ship and a man is sleeping on a chair. My dad smiles and says 'Don't wake him up; he's been on watch all night' and the man's sleep seems so deep as to be subterranean. I have no idea of this at the time, of course, but this introduction to the *Ark Royal* is my dad's farewell to the ocean, the ocean that has sustained him for two decades and through a world war during which he became my mother's pen pal and during which they met and got married because it was the war and you never knew what would happen.

We went to a tiny beach near a harbour and decades later I stand on that beach with my three children the night before a ferry trip to France. My middle daughter digs in the sand like I'm sure I must have done and my son sleeps in a buggy like maybe I did in my fictional pram. I feel a deep connection with the person I was and the people my parents were, as though I'm a kite and they're the string, or the other way round. The horizon is a long unbroken sentence.

Then, years later, I'm doing a gig in Plymouth and I stay in an old hotel and as I walk into the foyer I am overcome by a sudden wave of nostalgia and emotion because I am convinced that this is the hotel my mother and I stayed in when we came to see my dad in 1958; it can't be, can it? Surely so much will have changed since 1958 that I wouldn't notice anything, would I? Except maybe once you've been somewhere you leave something behind. In this case it's a memory of me talking and talking and talking in the hotel dining room, presumably at breakfast, and then I climb off my chair and go under the table and start to sing. My mother is embarrassed but a man says, in a loud voice that will admit no argument, 'Believe me, my dear, one day that boy will be Prime Minister!' I stand rigid in the foyer, afraid to check in because I feel I might break some kind of spell forever. The person behind the desk clears her throat.

In 1958, on the *Ark Royal* or perhaps in a cramped office onshore, my dad is signing some papers. There is a tear in his eye that, I am convinced, spills out on to his cheek. Somehow the tear rolls out of the room and trickles down the road or across the ship and drips into the water, where it becomes part of the sea.

JULY 2020: THERE'S A COUPLE THERE WITH MASKS ON

It's a warm day and there's a hint of socially distanced summer in the air. Restrictions have been lifted and my mother-in-law is trying to decide if she can go to her beloved caravan in Cleethorpes for a curtailed season; usually she'll be there from April until early October, cycling and swimming and going on the bus and kalling (grand old Yorkshire word) with her mates at the Knit 'n' Natter, or should it be knatter, although the site itself is open from March until the end of November.

This virus year she's been reduced to welcoming my wife and I first to her garden and then to a tiny space near her old coalhouse where she's set up a couple of chairs and where we talk endlessly about what it'll be like at the coast at that very moment. 'It'll be red hot in front of the van,' she'll say, 'if that bit of wind would drop.' We nod and eat slices of last year's Christmas cake.

Now it's July and a key has turned in the lockdown lock and we're taking my mother-in-law to her caravan for the day just to try it. Bear in mind that she's not been further than the end of her path since March, and this is a long journey. We swing out of the end of the street and head for the sea.

The A1 and the M18. Then the M180, that motorway built to serve some kind of Lincolnshire Powerhouse that we're still waiting for and which suddenly ends and becomes the A180 which is like driving across a piece of avant-garde percussive/ drone music. We comment that, as we approach the North Sea, the weather seems to be getting better; we try to say it aloud but the road is too noisy so we just say it as part of our internal monologue.

We drive through Grimsby and trundle into Cleethorpes; the sun has staked a claim on the sky. There are quite a few people about and they're wearing the usual array of East Coast clobber. There are people in shorts and tops that exemplify the word *skimpy*. There are old men in suits and flat caps but, incongruously, trainers as white as half-sucked Polo mints. There are people in overcoats walking directly behind people in hotpants and tops that exemplify the word *scanty*. As we slow down in the limping traffic, my mother-in-law says, from the back seat, 'There's a couple with masks on. And there's another one.' We pass a bus and there are masked people aboard. My mother-in-law is reassured by this: all is as usual, except it's masked.

The tide is out. Of course it is. This is Cleethorpes. I'm exaggerating a little but I'm 64 years old and I've been to Cleethorpes endlessly over the years and I've only ever seen the tide in five times. I'm exaggerating a little. Twelve times. The sea is so far out it's speaking Dutch. There's life here, though; there are people sitting out at cafés sipping lattes and there are people sitting out at pubs glugging beer. A man walking along the front is laughing so uproariously that he seems to be in danger of his face working loose.

We've downloaded a pass that we show to the man at the caravan park barrier and he waves us through. A masked queue waits outside the shop in the manner of polite bank robbers. We pass the touring field and my mother-in-law says, as she always does, 'Plenty of tourers in!' A ball is kicked high into the sky. And then we pull up at the side of the caravan. And maybe now the summer can begin, carefully, cautiously, masked and distanced. The two keys let us in; it doesn't seem like half an hour since we were locking up in October and looking forward to a new season that, we all reassured ourselves, might be the best one ever.

We sit and marvel that here we are again, that this little scrap of coast has welcomed my mother-in-law once more, like it has since the 1940s. So much has changed and yet the sky hasn't, and the sea, like a reluctant teenager, still doesn't want to come in.

We get the kettle on and we go for fish and chips. We know that if we ask for fish and chips three times we will get so many chips that my mother-in-law will be able to eat them until August, so we have three fish and just one portion of chips. A small portion, which still contains enough chips to feed Kettering and probably Corby too. Not Wellingborough though. That would be exaggerating.

We bring the fish and chips back to the caravan and my mother-in-law has buttered some bread and got the red and brown sauce out. So little in 2020 makes me happy; so much in 2020 makes me sad and angry but: these chips, these old plates, this buttered bread, this brown sauce, this crafted batter, the sound of a grass cutter in the distance, the sound of a gull laughing at its own joke, all make me happy.

We go for a walk on the tops and down to the sands, like we always do, and the tide turns like Columbo at the door and starts to wander in. My mother-in-law sees someone she knows from a nearby caravan and they exchange a few unmasked words. We stroll back for tea and cake, the vast truth of the sea to our backs.

In the caravan, my wife asks, 'Do you think you'll come back then, Mam? To stop?' My mother-in-law considers for a moment, but only for a moment. 'I think I will,' she says. I married into an undemonstrative but profoundly loving family and I know how much this means. There won't be swimming, of course, and there won't be bus trips and there will be no knitting and nattering but there will be a presence here, defiantly walking, slowly and with a stick, but defiantly walking by the distant sea. 'Shall I put the kettle on?' my mother-in-law says.

SEPTEMBER 2020: THE ETERNAL EPCOT FRIDGE MAGNET

I kid myself on, in reflective moments on settees and on masked journeys on trains, that as far as the coast goes, I want to visit new places, to feel the wind wrestle with my white hair as I look at vistas for the first time. I see myself as some kind of explorer, happening upon a slice of coast that has never felt the kiss of human feet before; I know that's unlikely in the UK but anything is possible in the world of my imagination as the song from *Willy Wonka and the Chocolate Factory* almost goes.

In the same way that my wife and I have pretended that we're going to visit every preserved steam railway and every private independent museum in the country, we sometimes entertain the fantasy that one day we'll walk all the way around the Coast Path, from Land's End to Land's End again. We had this idea just before the 2008 crash as we watched the tiny TV in our room in a hotel in Perranporth in Cornwall, mesmerised at people queuing up to get their money out of Northern Rock, and the next day, trading on the capital of wind and sun, we walked about four miles of the path and got chased by cows. Since then the ambition has lain dormant, although we have been on a few steam railways. Well, a couple. But, I've got all these areas of virgin coastal sand to walk on!

The fact is that I'm not really a pioneer and that for me the familiar parts of the coast are the most attractive; they're like earworms for the soul, their music stretching over time and space in comfort blankets that are made from the flux of coastal weather.

One of my favourite familiar stretches of the sea/land interface is Beadnell in Northumberland. I'll narrow it down: one of my favourite familiar stretches of the sea/land interface is that bit of Beadnell near the tiny harbour that, the minute you arrive there, someone will tell you is the only harbour on the East Coast that faces West and because you're charitable you have to pretend you'd not heard the fact before. I'll narrow it down some more: one of my favourite familiar stretches of the sea/land interface is that cottage in Beadnell near the tiny harbour not far from the dunes where we've stayed many times and the same fridge magnet has been on the fridge. The fridge has changed but the magnet hasn't, like a forest that's been completely cleared but somehow the carved initials of old lovers are still growing on the new saplings.

In the post-lockdown Covid autumn opening, my wife and I visited the cottage as we had over the years and as soon as I opened the door I glanced at the fridge and the EPCOT magnet was still there and it seemed that if I listened hard, the fridge was singing in harmony with the seabirds outside. I felt fulfilled and I was reminded of the moment in the Summer Loosening (as future historians will call it) when my three-year-old grandson Noah was allowed into our house for the first time for months. The first thing he did was to run through the house to check if the wooden badger that was awarded to me as BBC Wildlife Poet of the Year in 1992 was still there, and when it was, on top of the bookcase, he was happy. One boy's badger is another man's fridge magnet, as the old saying ought to go. We got the badger down from the top shelf where it lived and it seemed very pleased to see us.

I sat on the settee and faced the window that faced the dunes; a rabbit hopped across the lawn and greeted us warmly by dropping some droppings in a kind of wildlife version of the welcome mint on the pillow of an anonymous chain hotel. I turned to one side and saw that the Barbara Taylor Bradford novel was still there. I turned to the other side and saw that the painting of Seahouses Harbour was still there. I'm sure that last time we came the same rabbit had dropped (different) droppings.

Having confirmed that everything was as close to being the same as it could be, we set off to walk towards the harbour that in some brochures might be called boutique. As we strolled and a gull laughed at us, we both noticed that although some things hadn't changed, a number of other things had. There were bright yellow skips everywhere, full of resting wood and plaster held in abeyance. One held an incongruous candlestick, another displayed a set of pre-loved dining chairs. Old properties were being rebuilt in all directions like some kind of Festival of the Breeze Block. One place in particular was, in the Hollywood actor kind of way, having some work done so that even the house next door might not recognise it in the dark.

There's the dilemma of the tourist like me who just wants to sit on those chairs and look at that candlestick. We don't want change and we want things to stay exactly the same and in the same place like that Barbara Taylor Bradford book. This, though, is surely wrong; places have to be allowed to breathe and change just as the coast breathes and changes. My attachment to this place is sentimental because I've spent quite a slice of my life there, and it fits me like a cardigan.

We carry on to the harbour. The ice-cream van is there and we buy ice creams because we always do on our first walk. A man stands near us and we strike up the kind of weather/virus conversation that is being struck up everywhere in 2020. He points at the water and I know what he's going to say but I let him say it anyway because it's part of the holiday ritual after all. He harboursplains: 'Did you know that Beadnell Harbour is the only harbour on the East Coast that faces West?' I feign amazement. Maybe a little too enthusiastically. There is accidental ice cream on my chin.

MARCH 2020: THE LOST GLOVE AND THE HIGH WIND

Scarborough: proper Yorkshire seaside, tha knows. Like Blackpool with curd tart and parkin or like Barnsley overlaid with a beach. In early March 2020, as the virus seemed to be simultaneously very close and very far away, my wife and I took a trip to Scarborough to prepare ourselves for what we both thought would be a very memorable year. How right/wrong/right/wrong we were.

The train wasn't very busy as it rolled into the station but yet in a sense it was because whenever you get out of your carriage at this particular end of the line you're jostled and shoved aside and almost knocked over by the vast crowds of people who have visited the town over the years. There they are, in their Sunday best or their beachy worst, wielding buckets and spades like they are weapons in a kind of benevolent war. Their laughter is infectious and they've supped a couple and they're ready to leave the pit and the factory and the mill behind and just have some fun of the kind that sprays itself all over the place and sings at inappropriate times, whatever they are. Of course there's a gentle, broadsheet side to Scarborough too but the terrible racket invariably drowns it out and that's part of its attraction.

When I was a younger man, I heard a tale about Scarborough that sums up part of its slapstick beauty; in the story (which may or may not be true but because it's set at the seaside, who really cares? Was The Ancient Mariner true? I rest my case. On the guest-house steps.) a boy gets separated from his parents in the teeming sandopolis of the beach. We've all done it: one moment we are within the familiar orbit of the nurturing parental planet and the next we are at the edge of the universe moving among beings we don't recognise as human. Especially with those Lancashire accents. The boy glances up and can't see his mam or dad. He does what any reasonable human being would do: he wets himself and runs shouting across the sands. Then six legs begin to run towards him at once from the other end of the beach. Two belong to the boy's father and four belong to an escaped donkey. I would like to believe that the donkey was called Bravo, but that's just a detail of the story I've made up so that I can imagine people shouting Bravo! Bravo! to the donkey as it runs. The father looks as though he's either chasing the donkey or competing with it in a Dads 'n' Donkeys race at a summer fete.

The boy is running towards both the donkey and his dad and it looks for a moment as though there will be what sports commentators call a coming together. The boy is still damp and inconsolable and the donkey, perhaps sensing this, runs straight past him. In the distance, by the way, some elderly people are trying to catch the donkey too. Maybe they wanted a ride.

The dad catches up with the boy and whispers to him, that special kind of whispering that stops tears, lifting him up and pointing at the running donkey as if to say that donkey was lost too but soon it will find a friend. The boy smiles a fragile porcelain smile. The dad carries the child on his shoulders in triumph towards the donkey, which has donkey-blundered its way through a throng of people. It seems that the throng is growing and becoming raucous. People are pointing. Some are looking away.

The dad carries the boy to the front of the crowd; they part to let him through. Some of them are parting mischievously but the boy and his dad don't know that yet.

Ah. Now they do. The donkey has found a friend. The donkey has found a close and very special friend and is showing affection in a very physical way. The bells around his head are jingling rhythmically. Perhaps, like the rest of us, the donkey was just running to find love. With bells on.

The beach will have to wait for another day for my wife and I because today we want to walk to the castle. I think I know a back way and it turns out that in a kind of 'back way via the back way' I do. We keep seeing the castle but we don't seem to be getting any closer to it. The wind has got up, presumably after a late night. It begins to tug at my clothes like it wants something. The castle teases us, hiding behind trees and terraced streets. Eventually, blown by the wind, we find it. It is as though the wind is some kind of fussy relative we have brought with us, one of those relatives who is always nudging you to tell you something really, really interesting.

We go to the little hut to pay and the wind is rocking it. The English Heritage person warns us that parts of the castle are closed to visitors because of the high winds and she has to speak up because the winds are so high and she ends up speaking in harmony with the winds.

We step out of the hut and into the wind. Our shadows are blown away instantly. My wife reaches into her pocket to put her gloves on and discovers that they are not there. We walk out of the castle to retrace our steps and the woman from the hut asks where we're going because, like disgruntled guests at a party, we've only just arrived.

We walk along, looking at the floor. I imagine the gloves far out at sea, waving and later drowning. It feels like the wind is laughing at us. It feels like this coastal day will be tarnished and rusty before it has really got going.

And then we find the gloves holding hands, one with a thumb up. They almost seem to move together in the gathering gale. And I think about the donkey. And I laugh.

YEARS WENT OVER AND NOBODY FOUND US

The man who passed me on a coastal path in Scotland and said 'Who knows that the sea knows, eh?' and carried on walking before I could reply, which was a good job because I couldn't think of a reply. The boy who was standing on a bench near the beach at Cleethorpes doing magic tricks in front of a tiny audience and the wind blew his hat off but he carried on doing the tricks. The man who broke wind symphonically and deafeningly as he walked with his wife past some amusements in Filey and who, as his wife told him off in a hissing sibilant paragraph of rage, sang 'Better out than in' in a fine operatic tenor.

The man who asked me, as the sea battered Bridlington Harbour, if I'd seen his magnet. 'It's shaped like a magnet' he said, not smiling. The woman sitting on a deckchair at Skegness who had fallen asleep so spectacularly that all her bones seemed to have deserted her; she was liquid. The man who chased a kite down a beach that is just that in my memory; a beach. He is distinctive and the kite is distinctive but the beach is a beach.

The family who stood around a jellyfish at the edge of Seahouses Harbour; they, and the jellyfish, were perfectly still and the jellyfish looked like a fallen planet and they could have been moons in shorts. The gull that came in through the open window of my hotel room in St Ives and sat on the end of my bed regarding me with an intelligence that seemed superior to mine; I lunged to cover up the complementary biscuit. The time my son threw a message in a bottle into the sea and it went out a little way and then came back in a few yards down the beach and a boy grabbed it and opened it and shouted excitedly to his dad 'There's somebody called Andrew who lives in Barnsley and who wants to write to somebody!' and my son and I kept quiet and looked in the other direction but a letter never came.

The bus driver who shouted 'The brakes are away!' as the old coach rattled down to Tobermory Harbour; somehow it slowed down just before the water, unlike my heart. The posh family on a beach who said that they couldn't possibly open the hamper until Mrs T arrived; I assumed she was a family friend but she was the servant. They applauded when she arrived and she opened the wicker door and solemnly gave out napkins. They sprayed each other with champagne but it was a genteel spray; one of them clicked their fingers at Mrs T and she passed them a clean napkin.

The man in the black suit who lay on the beach at Scarborough like he was on a funeral director's away day; he was not dead, only sleeping, and a black dog lay at his feet. The words MAY MAY I LOVE YOU MAY on a beach in Wales, being eaten by the slow unsentimental tide. The man who shouted 'Jump, Green Trousers!' as I hesitated to leap from a pitching and rolling boat on to the island of Lundy; I was certainly wearing green trousers and my breakfast was tattooed on my jumper. The man who pointed at the T-shirt I was wearing on the sands one summer; I thought I was being clever and a bit subversive by getting the words JUGS OF SAND FOR THE TEA printed on it at one of those booths that seemed to be everywhere in those days. He carried on pointing and said, 'That should be "jugs of tea for the sand" you know.' I bit back a sharp retort and carried on walking, my irony flapping in the wind.

My children playing a game on the beach at New Quay in Wales; it involved me bringing them a note and then walking away and them saying 'Years went over and nobody found us'; to this day, decades later, I still well up when I think about that moment. The man in tightly fitting shorts who ran past me at Bamburgh and shouted 'Keep writing them poems' and he was way past me before he could register my raised thumb and my nod of the head. The wicked grin on the face of the woman who was helping her children bury her husband in the sand; his comb-over was like seaweed in the sun and his smile was just this side of forced. Her smile was determined, as she piled on more sand than was strictly necessary. There was a story there that William Trevor or VS Pritchett could have written. In my fading memory of the event one of the children was called Rollo but maybe I made that up. My Uncle Jack trying to hypnotise me on the short ferry ride to Caldy Island in South Wales by swinging his watch in front of my face and saying 'You're leaving. You're on your way. You're leaving…'

My dad buying me a Cornish pasty in Bridlington that I didn't really want because, although I'd never had one before, the nascent poet in me thought that the word 'pasty' rhymed with the word 'nasty' so it wouldn't taste very nice so I dropped it in the harbour where it made a pasty/nasty splash and I told my dad what had happened and he bought me another one, which wasn't the climax to my plan that I'd envisaged.

Shaking enough sand out of my shoes over the years to make at least one beach, with the tide way, way out. The sand spreads across the floor and across my memory. Maybe that's what memory is: a tide that goes out and then comes in with things floating and swimming in it. Things to remember. Things to write down and keep forever. Years went over and nobody found us.

THE HELICOPTER AT THE PICNIC

Many years ago I did a performance at the wonderful Alnwick Playhouse in Northumberland; I read my poems and told stories and it seemed to go down quite well. I noticed, on the front row, a woman a little bit older than me who kept nudging the young boy next to her to get him to at least look at me and stop gazing around the room. The boy was having none of it; he was at the stage of spectacular and performative boredom that children sometimes get to when they're taken/dragged/cajoled along to an event that isn't really suitable for them. Not that there's any *adult content* at any of my gigs but sometimes the language might be a little over their heads. They often squirm as though they are the captain of the UK squirming team and their sighs are the subject of emergency calls to the Noise Abatement Society. In the end he just sat there eating a pillowcase-sized bag of crisps.

As the show carried on (because the show must go on), I began to realise that I vaguely recognised the woman but I couldn't really place her. After the show I saw her in the foyer and she came up and introduced herself: 'Do you remember?' she said, as the boy tugged at her arm so that they could escape this strange place. 'You and your family stayed on the upper floor of my house in Boulmer in the 1980s, and one night I saw you on the telly and I said to my husband "that's the man upstairs" and so ever since then you've been the man upstairs.' I did remember, then, and the years fell away like a tottering pile of cards. The boy had almost dragged her away by now but she turned at the door and said 'And you had a helicopter at your picnic, remember?'

And I'd forgotten the helicopter, but then it came back, vivid as rotor blades in the sun. That night in a bland hotel room I dreamed of the helicopter and the beach and I woke up sweating and had to make a cup of tea and the kettle sounded too loud for the room's tight geometry. Maybe the beaches and shorelines we visit when our children are small are always going to have a dream-like quality and they are going to be lit by sea-light. Maybe any rain that falls will be a kind of healing rain and the sunny moments will be the ones that imprint themselves in your mind forever, like sandal prints on sand that somehow never get washed away and that somehow are still there when you go back, no matter how long it is between visits.

It was 1987 and I remember that I was probably the only person in the UK who thought that Labour were going to win the election. It was held on 11 June, which was five days after my elder daughter's fourth birthday and my younger daughter's second birthday because they were twins, two years apart. That's what they call family planning in Barnsley. I sat up all night drinking cheap red wine and hoping for a late surge from the Midlands that never quite appeared and the next morning, groggy and disappointed, my wife and I took the children for a picnic on the beach. I was the groggy one; they'd slept well.

We got to the beach at Boulmer and the drizzle was more or less invisible. More or less. I took the girls down to the water and we indulged in some synchronised splashing and pro-celebrity laughing while my wife spread a picnic blanket on the sand and filled it with hope and optimism and crisps. A buggy held down one corner of the blanket and stones secured the others. She waved at us and we wandered back to start the joyful ritual.

In the distance, like a surge in the Midlands, an item of punctuation resolved itself into a helicopter from nearby RAF Boulmer. The girls and I walked up the beach and I pointed out the helicopter and I told the girls to wave even though, somehow, I associated helicopters with the kind of military might that had helped the Conservatives to flatten everything in front of them in the election. Wheeling gulls were still, for a moment, bigger than the helicopter.

We got to the picnic and we sat down to start to eat. For a brief moment we didn't know where the helicopter was, but we could still hear its droning song, which seemed to be all chorus and no verse. Suddenly, as though we were in a film about the Falklands War, we saw the helicopter racing at a height that experts would describe as 'not very high' down the beach towards our little group. The girls, innocently, still waved.

The helicopter, and time itself, seemed to stop. It hovered like a science fiction insect. It zoomed vertically, moved a little through the Northumberland air, and began to hover again, this time directly over our picnic. The picnic blanket began to shake and shiver, and then it took off. Crisps flew. Sandwiches tried to take cover. The buggy fell. I shook my stupid fist at the helicopter and after a while it buzzed away, eventually becoming a speck again.

I'm back in my hotel room in Alnwick and I'm drinking tea. It's the middle of the night and an ambulance passes. After we'd tried to rescue our picnic it started to drizzle again and we walked back to the cottage where we met the woman who'd recognised me off the TV and we told her the story of what had just happened.

The boy she'd brought to my gig wasn't born, of course, but maybe she'd told him the tale of the picnic blanket that flapped like a mainsail in a storm and me standing there like Captain Ahab shaking a feeble fist at something huge and scary. Maybe the lad expected my show to be just as exciting. Sorry.

Still, the memory's there now, always hovering just above any picnic I'll ever have.

PIECES TO CAMERA

As I'm finding as I'm writing the pages that make up this book like grains of sand make up a beach, when you have to put your feelings about the coast down on paper, they somehow try to flit away and become oddly ungraspable. For me the coast, the sea's sandy sleeve, is something that's truly and fundamentally indefinable and so any rendering of it into prose or poetry will give it a solidity and narrative arc that maybe it doesn't really have. That's the glory and the frustration of art, I guess, and that's why a description of a gull shitting on your chips isn't as visceral as the actual chip-shitting moment.

If writing about the coast is one way of simultaneously capturing it and realising you can never capture it, then talking to a camera about it is another layer of that dilemma. For a start, you've got to light the chips properly and mic up the gull.

I made a few little films for the BBC show *Coast* and that taught me how to tell a place's story succinctly and how to talk to a camera over my shoulder while not tripping up.

We went to Whitby to tell the story of the *Rohilla* Disaster, a tragedy that happened in the First World War when a boat sank just a few hundred yards off the coast but rescuers couldn't get to the sinking vessel because of the terrible storm that rattled and raged and yelled across the sky. All kinds of methods were attempted to get people back to land but sadly many people died. Before the filming I met the director in a café far from the sea and I sipped espresso in an attempt to look more sophisticated than I felt.

'How do you feel about heights?' she asked. I said I was OK with heights, but at the same time wondering just what was coming next. She said, 'How do you feel about zip wires?' I drank my espresso in what I hoped was a nonchalant fashion, although the tuba-style gulping noises I was making might have betrayed my state of mind. 'I'm OK with zip wires,' I said, with a sob in my voice. She explained that one of the rescue methods they attempted in 1914 was to get people to sit in leather breeches and haul them from the *Rohilla* on a zip wire. I joked that I couldn't see myself in leather breeches and that I'd probably look like Ross Geller in *Friends* when he tried some on. She glanced at her phone and the meeting was suddenly over as she went out of the café.

I told my wife about the leather breeches and the zip wire and she laughed more than I thought she would. I spent sleepless nights sweating about the zip and dreaming about it during nano-seconds of fitful slumber. I thought about pulling out. Of the filming not the breeches. Then the director rang and said they'd abandoned the leather breeches plan due to 'health and safety concerns' and in my palpitating relief I said 'I didn't want to breach those rules' and the silence at the end was like that of a stuffed wading bird in a museum. Then she said that because I wouldn't be zipping down the wire, I'd be required to row a lifeboat out to sea. I almost wept with relief.

So there I am at the very edge of Whitby Harbour speaking to a camera as a huge vintage lifeboat bobs in the water like an apple in that old Halloween game. Myself and the other stout-thewed volunteers are going to row the boat out to where the *Rohilla* sank; it's to be a solemn moment at the end of a solemn piece but because we're filming out of sequence this is the first solemnity. Whitby's raucousness seems to dim as I speak to the lens and even the gulls seem to be mournful rather than sceptical. Luckily the sea is mournful rather than angry because I'd told a little white lie to the director when she'd asked me if I was a good sailor. My dad, the old salt, would have been ashamed of me, but I'm not. Even a slight bump in a carpet nudges me towards the foothills of biliousness. 'As long as you keep your eyes on the horizon you'll be OK,' my dad used to say, and he'd kept his eyes on more horizons than most.

I climb down the steps to the lifeboat. My life jacket is bulky and the microphone is sticking to my back. I'm like an actor in a fat suit. I take up the oar, which seems like a caber or a mighty oak. I can hardly move it. One of the volunteers, a man much older than me, turns and says, 'Don't let us down, Ian.' The director and the camera operative and the sound person climb aboard too. The boat shifts, grumbling.

We begin to row out of the harbour. I achieve a kind of stumbling rhythm as though I am the token older Z-list celebrity on *Strictly Come Dancing* but then, as we approach the harbour wall, I realise that somebody has set fire to my shoulders and arms. I deliver a piece to camera and I try to keep the grimace out of my voice. Here I am, explaining the sea to itself. Seasplaining. Iansplaining. We are almost out of the harbour, where I know, from memories of childhood trips on pleasure boats in Bridlington, the real fun will begin. I've stood on harbour walls many times watching families gaily laughing and drinking pop and eating crisps as they smooth their way to the open sea, where things change and the PG trip becomes an 18.

As we turn out of the harbour into the melee (and it's not even windy, remember) I have to start asking the skipper some questions. The air is calm and that means that we can all hear my barber from Darfield, the late Mad Geoff, shout 'Give him twenty lashes! Avast behind!' The moment is shattered. 'Did you get that?' the director asks the sound man. He nods. Later, over a coffee, he will tell me that he is, like me, a fan of avant-garde music and found sounds. Maybe not that particular found sound.

We have to row in a circle (Seven words. Easy to write. Hard to achieve.) and then I have to ask the question again. Luckily, Mad Geoff has wandered off.

We row out to sea. It isn't, in my memory, too bad. I don't feel sick. I ask the questions and do a couple more pieces to camera. We turn round and, to the relief of my tortured body, we begin to head back. 'Where's the other boat?' the director asks. The camera operative points it out, a tiny vessel like a toy in a bath. I ask what the other boat is for, which betrays my lack of deep knowledge of the film-making process. Of course there's no point just filming on one boat because the viewers never see the boat in full, so my rowing prowess and interviewing skills have to be filmed from another boat.

In other words, we have to do it again. Not all of it; just most of it. Give him twenty lashes. At least I wasn't on a zip wire.

THE COAST THAT WASN'T A COAST OR MAYBE IT WAS

It's 1964 and I'm walking home from Low Valley Junior School with my mate Keith Barlow. The school is in the valley, the low valley, and we're walking up the long hill; the valley is misty but there is sun, enfeebled but strengthening, at the top of the hill on Barnsley Road. A bloke walks towards us and it's obvious to me now from a distance of many decades, even though it wasn't at the time, that he's spent a few hours and a few quid in The Darfield Hotel. His steps are tentative and leaning towards the turbulent. I'm writing this in the present tense because it is always present to me in my head; later I'll do a gear change to the past tense as I try to peer through the lens of history.

'Heyop lads!' he shouts, his voice enlivened by a win on the fruit machine. 'Look down theer!' He points to the mist-laden valley, past the school to Darfield Main Pit and the headgear that looks as though it's been drawn on a theatrical backdrop with a pencil. Although I'm familiar with the headgear and the winding wheels, perhaps I'm too familiar with them; they're just part of the landscape, something I never think about.

'Look!' he shouts again, too loud for the muffled afternoon. 'Blackpool Tower!' He points theatrically, too theatrically. He almost falls over. I look; yes, that could be Blackpool Tower. It really could. Keith Barlow says, 'But isn't that the pit?' The drunk bloke's face almost slides to the ground in amazement, cartoon fashion. 'Nay, kid. That's Blackpool Tower. Get down theer and have a paddle,' and he wanders off, laughing.

Keith Barlow and I discussed the sudden appearance of Blackpool Tower as we walked home: could it be true? Could there really be the seaside down where the River Dove ambled towards the River Dearne? We parted at the top of the hill and decided to investigate at the weekend. *Dr Who* had recently arrived on our tiny black-and-white TV screens and the programme had opened up all kinds of temporal and spatial possibilities for the people who watched it, like it still does. In other words, it didn't seem odd that Blackpool Tower might suddenly materialise in the middle of the South Yorkshire Coalfield.

My dad, a practical man with a hint of the romantic, was dismissive; he said that it couldn't possibly be Blackpool Tower. Then he paused and said 'It might just be a trick of the light', which led me to believe that maybe he thought it was possible. My mother, a romantic woman with a hint of the practical, was gently enthusiastic: 'Well, it might be. All kind of things can happen in this world.' Which led me to believe that it really was happening and that the seaside could be anywhere you wanted it to be.

We couldn't wait until the weekend; the next day at school we told our teacher Mrs Hudson about what we'd seen and because this was a West Riding Education Authority School where Creativity was everything, she told us to write a poem about it. At playtime, from the yard, we were disappointed not to be able to see the tower. It wasn't misty any more so surely it should have been in plain sight, but it wasn't. In the bright sun the River Dove shone like a bread knife. A gull passed over on its way to the tip, giving us a moment of brief hope. The pithead gear of Darfield Main was just that: the pithead gear of Darfield Main. The wheels were turning, bringing a shift up the shaft or dropping a shift down to the face and from this distance of years

I can imagine that a lot of those men wished they were paddling in Blackpool rather than coughing dust in Yorkshire.

The next day Keith and I told our parents that we had some after-school activities and we'd be a little late home. This was both true and not true; they weren't official activities like the Chess Club or tidying the school garden, they were unofficial coastline-hunting activities.

We walked out of school that afternoon and Mrs Gaskell the lollipop lady showed us across the road. As an aside, I sometimes think that one of the reasons I'm a writer is that I had a lollipop lady called Mrs Gaskell; when I left the Juniors in 1967 to go to The Big School I gave her my autograph book to sign and she wrote 'Well done is better than well said'; that sounded impressive and I said so but then she pointed to the same words on a poster on the wall of the Methodist chapel opposite. The reason she's in a book about the coast is that I saw her many years later walking round the harbour in Bridlington. I walked up to her and declared 'Well done is better than well said' but her face was as blank as an eggshell.

Keith and I wandered down Pit Street to the pit. Huge wagons of coal trundled by and the pit bus rattled along, taking the morning shift home. The pit gear loomed in the bright afternoon. It didn't look much like Blackpool Tower but we pretended that it did, in the same way we pretended that we could see Stephenson's *Rocket* when we went trainspotting down by the sidings.

A kind of fiction-generating madness overcame us. We saw the Tower. We saw trams. We saw donkeys. We saw people in Kiss Me Quick hats eating bags of chips. The idea that the coast could somehow transpose itself to the middle of the country didn't occur to us as odd because in our imagination anything was possible, anything at all. We even believed we'd made a sandcastle, in the dirt by the pit pond.

And then, just like it was time for tea at a guest house, we went to our separate homes and never spoke about it again, until now, because The Coast is a coast of the mind as well as something that gets between your toes.

OVEREXPOSURE

Picture my Uncle Charlie: a tall man, dapper in braces and high-waisted trousers. Picture his three flat caps: garden, house and best. Picture his glasses, the lenses thick as smog. Uncle Charlie couldn't read or write; as a boy, I once tried to teach him but the childish books I used (I was a child, after all) embarrassed us both and the lessons ended when he stood up, spat into the fire and said 'I'm going to the darkroom, lad. You can come if you want but leave the books out here.'

Charlie's darkroom, fashioned out of the coal shed by the back door of his house, was his pride and joy. We would sit in there for hours, sometimes lit by a sunrise of a red light as he developed and printed photographs, his pit-shattered lungs rasping like waves on a shingle beach. The moment he liked best was the magical time when the prints began to appear in the tray of liquid. It was like cave paintings were emerging from the gloom, lit by the candles of nineteenth-century explorers. It's true to say, though, that his black-and-white images often turned out to be more white than black, and that's the way he liked it. It was as though the bleached images were the opposite of the coal face down Houghton Main, that their shiny emptiness acted as antidotes to that dusty darkness he spent so much of his time in.

Charlie and his wife, Auntie, came on holiday with us quite often in those days, and he would snap away happily on beaches, promenades, clifftops and smoky cafés, develop the photographs at home and then keep them in a Quality Street tin, which he kept in a cupboard in the kitchen. Because he couldn't read or write he didn't write the location of each photo on the back so the tin was a map of mysteries that none of us could unravel.

That didn't seem to matter so much when they were in the tin but one Christmas he got a photograph album and Auntie (her name was Gladys but we called her Auntie unless we called her Tanty) persuaded him to stick his photos in and enlisted me to write some captions. We emptied the tin over the kitchen table and set to work.

Or we tried to. We held one up; it was a glossy and almost entirely bleached image, that, if you looked really closely, appeared to be a caravan perched on a cliff. I used a phrase I'd recently heard someone use on the TV and said, 'It's overexposed.' Charlie's response was a variation on his usual phrase, said in mock-threatening tones: 'You'll be overexposed in a minute!' Auntie picked the print up and stared at it, then she wiped it on her floral pinny and looked at it again. 'It's that place near Llandudno,' she said, with an air of finality. 'I recognise that fence.' 'What fence, Mrs Woman?' said Charlie. 'I can't see a fence, and nor can Clem Attlee here.' He pointed at me; he often referred to me as Clem Attlee, or Stirling Moss, or Souse, or Jim's Dad's Hoss, none of which made any sense to me, but were probably, somehow, part of the reason I've always enjoyed working at the language face.

Auntie squinted. 'There's a fence. It was near Llandudno. Remember, we went to Llandudno and we went up that Great Home on the tram.' Welsh readers are right to be appalled at Auntie's pronunciation of Llandudno and her rendering of The Great Orme.

Here is an area of the coast that a book blurb would call 'shrouded in mystery' because none of us knew where it was. If a photograph is a representation of a moment in time then maybe it doesn't matter that we don't know where it is, maybe the fact that Uncle Charlie took the snap is enough. The three of us stand looking at the almost completely overexposed picture; the light through the window tries its best to turn us into people in a Renaissance painting but the flat cap and the pinny are too much for the comparison to hold for more than a few seconds.

The door opens and my mother and dad come in; they've just been to the shop and my dad is carrying a white loaf and my mother is carrying an Aero, which she hands to me.

Uncle Charlie doesn't waste time. He points to the print and says 'Where's that?' My dad holds it up and says 'Watchet'. He passes it to my mother and says the word Watchet again because I know he loves saying the word. She gazes at it for a long time. Uncle Charlie says 'Llandudno. Near Llandudno' as though in some parallel universe Llandudno is near Llandudno. Auntie says 'The Great Home'. My mother turns the print around, then turns it around again as though any way you look at the photo it is upside down.

Maybe we all have a coast of the mind that we keep in safekeeping for when we need it most; maybe the fact that we are seeing different parts of the coast and mining them from the same photograph is what makes the coast so special. It can be anywhere, for anybody. 'Plymouth' my mother says, with an air of finality.

Mrs Beck from next door comes in to give my auntie some *People's Friend*s that she's finished with, and we try to rope her in to guessing the mystery resort but she says, with a voice steeped in Park Drives and crispy bacon, 'I'm not starting that game', which is a shame, because I recall that morning at 34 North Street as a moment of great joy, a brief time when it didn't matter where the picture was taken, just that it was taken at all. That coast could have been any coast and it could have been every coast. The Great Home, as Auntie would have said.

SIX AND OUT

Steve's raring to go; he's only just arrived at my mother-in-law's caravan in Cleethorpes and he's raring to go. The rest of us are having a cup of coffee and a biscuit from the tin under the bed but Steve is getting the bat and the ball and the stumps out of the car boot. 'Come on! Beach cricket!' he says. We say we'll meet him on the dunes and he sets off with my grandson Thomas, pushing my little granddaughter Isla in the buggy, which would be 'a bit of a tow', as we say round these parts, once they get to the sands. Me and my wife and Elizabeth, who is Isla and Thomas's mum and Steve's wife, have another biscuit and then Kate, my other daughter, and her husband Mark arrive so the kettle goes on again. Then it goes on again when my son Andrew and his partner Ben arrive. The caravan windows steam up and there are archipelagos of crumbs across the floor.

Steve texts Elizabeth. 'He says are we coming. He says where are we?' We decide to set off for our epic game of beach cricket that we've been promising ourselves for weeks. 'Are you coming, Mam?' my wife says. 'Of course I am!' she replies, reaching for her stick. It's not that warm out there so it takes us ages to get our coats back on and then we set off, like pilgrims, to the beach.

Steve is ready and he's got Thomas bowling to him. Isla is asleep. In a couple of years' time Steve and I will be at Headingley watching Ben Stokes defeat the mighty Australians on his own at that epic test match, and because I get tremendously emotional when I'm watching sport, I spend much of the time with my head in my hands trying not to look; and what is swirling around in my head as Steve shouts 'Look, man! We're witnessing history here!' is that beautiful game of beach cricket that seemed to be built from love, and sand, and sea breezes and shared jokes, and strong family ties.

Steve's ready. He picks me. Thomas picks Mark. Steve picks my wife. Thomas picks his mum. Steve picks Kate. Mark picks Ben. Steve picks Andrew. Isla wakes up. Mark picks Isla. Steve bowls to Mark who knocks the ball far away, into the sea, which is very far away because this is Cleethorpes. A distant dog's bark appears to be built from scornful laughter. 'You can't knock it that far!' my wife says. 'You'll lose the ball!' my mother-in-law says. So we agree that the strokes will be more gentle, more skilful.

I stroll every morning and I do exercises so I think I'm fit; the year before, in our cottage in Beadnell on the Northumberland coast, I announced to my wife that I was going to go running each morning, even though I never ran anywhere unless it was to a bus stop to catch the X19. It was a serious mistake. Running for exercise is very different from running to the bus stop. I trickle-trundled across the vast sands just before dawn like a chess piece moved by a player who knows that the game is already lost. I limped back to the cottage; if I had been a character in the *Beano*, the word OUCH would have been hovering over my head like a drone. My wife shook her head; I would have made a smart-alec reply but I was in too much pain although I realise that you don't talk with feet. It was just that the pain was dancing all the way from my feet to my head.

So that is why I'm a little cautious when it comes to my turn to bat in the glorious festival of improvisation that is beach cricket. Thomas is ready to bowl at me; Thomas is in his early teenage years at this point and he's a good cricketer who takes lots of wickets at Darfield where the enthusiastic sledging of the youth teams is a joy: 'He's got more leaves than a tree!' one of them will always shout as a batsman lets a ball glide by. 'Be gentle, Thomas!' my wife shouts, noticing the gleam in Thomas's eye. 'I'm ready for owt!' I shout, with vim and braggadocio, or the Barnsley equivalent of braggadocio which is brussenness.

Thomas takes a long run-up that takes him almost to Freeman Street Market in Grimsby, where my mother-in-law buys eggs and vegetables from a stall, and where, with her mate Margaret, she haunts the charity shops. (My mother-in-law is called Margaret too. Their shopping trip is a Margaret duet.) He pounds towards me across the sand.

It's a clear day; sometimes a cravat of mist hangs around Cleethorpes and sometimes reading the far horizon is like trying to read the bottom line of an optician's chart but that isn't the case this morning. The two forts, Bull Fort and Haile Fort, built to keep German shipping away from the Humber in the First World War, gleam in the sun. A huge ferry seems to walk across the surface of the water so slowly as to seem to be hardly moving at all.

Cricket gives you sublime moments, like that time at Headingley that I hardly dared to watch, and like these sublime moments on that beach with Thomas about to hurl the ball at me. He releases the ball and it zooms towards me with, as they say in the sports pages, 'unerring accuracy'. Usually the ball is a blur, a hyperblur, an uberblur, but this time the ball seems to be moving slowly through the salty air. They say this happens to elite sportspeople all the time; the football, the cricket ball, the rugby ball, the snooker ball seem to begin to travel like snails so that the elite sportsperson (in this case, me) can have plenty of time to decide not only what they want to do but also have a rummage through the free basket outside one of the charity shops on Freeman Street and come back with a grapefruit spoon.

I step forward into the shot and hit the ball as hard as I can and it flies high into the air and all the family watch it rise; my mother-in-law, my wife, my children, my grandchildren, all the people who help to define who I am and who I'd like to become.

And here's a thing; because the coast is a magical place where amazing things can happen between the turning of the tides and in the clink of a charity shop teacup, the ball never comes down. We wait, and we wait, and we look into the sky and the ball doesn't appear and so we walk back to the caravan to make a list of fish and chips orders, every now and then glancing upwards.

THE SAXOPHONE, THE SEA

Sometimes there are places that are so sacred you want to keep them to yourself because if somebody else got to know about them they might crack and eventually shatter; it's like letting somebody into your morning rituals that are built for you and only you. How would somebody else be able to fathom why you do those sit-ups lying on the living room floor or why you listen for the central heating coming on like a cellist might listen for the note before the one they are about to play?

It's like that with me and Cleethorpes; my wife's family have an almost umbilical attachment to it built from memories of splashing and sandcastles and donkey rides in happier, simpler times. I have grown to love it as I've taken my children and grandchildren there and watched them build their own donkey/splash/sandcastle memories.

So when, sometimes, my professional life takes me to Cleethorpes, I have to steel myself to let people into the private and sandy room in my soul, I have to hold a little bit of myself back, keep it safe for when I return. A few years ago I presented an evening for Radio 3 based around the idea of the sea, and produced by the great poet of nature writing Tim Dee; he asked me where I'd like to go to make a little ten-minute feature to insert into the evening and one of the places I mentioned was Cleethorpes and I almost instantly regretted the decision because I would be letting light in on magic.

I said that I'd like to wander along the sands and improvise a kind of spoken word piece about that part of the East Coast, and because I was given more or less free rein I'd said I'd like to invite the great jazz saxophonist Snake Davis along to improvise around my words and maybe perform some duets with any gulls who happened to be passing in search of chip-bounty.

We met Snake and his son on the seafront; there was a slight breeze, as there always is at Cleethorpes, and it melded with Snake warming up his instrument as his son sat on a bench and filled in a colouring book. Tim recorded it. The music and the colouring; when you're making this kind of what's now called Slow Radio, you record everything and shape it later, just like history does.

I walked up to one of those otherworldly telescopes that you put a pound in and then you can gaze at the horizon until you've had your money's worth. It worked, which in my experience is unusual, but it also creaked spectacularly, like a pub sign in a high wind.

I looked at Snake and he put his saxophone to his mouth and began a duet with the telescope as I rattled it around on its axis. I'm a fan of avant-garde music, the kind of noise that empties the room, and let me tell you that this was in the vanguard of the avant-garde. It was off-season in Cleethorpes and there were very few people around to witness this world premiere (and last ever performance) apart from a man in a hi-vis jacket who rode by on his bike and rang his bell enthusiastically, adding to the soundscape. It felt exhilarating and sublime and somehow it also felt that because it was so unusual it didn't threaten to pop the bubble of my family memories of the place; it felt self-contained, as though I was looking at it through a very different telescope to the one I normally gazed at the resort through.

We decided to walk to the sea and record me talking about the sound of the waves to the accompaniment of the saxophone; because the tide was out, this involved a walk that almost took us into another time zone. Eventually we arrived at the edge of the sea; it was fairly quiet, although some wrinkles in its face told us that it might have turned, that it might be coming back in.

Snake took a Japanese flute out of his bag and began to play; the tune was so beautiful that even the occasional cloud that smudged the sky seemed to be listening. As Snake played and the waves whispered, and I described the scene in hushed John Arlott-like tones, another sound began to impinge on our consciousness; a buzzing, rattling sound, as though a tiny bee had made a miniature music box but had somehow got themselves trapped inside. Snake played. The tide played. The noise got louder. The breeze seemed to lift it into the air and because of that we all looked up, expecting to see a light plane.

Suddenly Snake's son pointed; a jeep was zooming across the sand towards us. We were disappointed; the moment had been broken and Snake stopped playing. We thought the jeep would be packed with young joyriders intent on tearing the silence to pieces but it wasn't. The driver was the only occupant and he was a lifeguard.

'Come on, the tide's coming in! You'll be cut off!' he shouted. Tim recorded his words and the roar of the jeep and then we looked around and the tide was indeed wandering in; indeed, it was doing more than wandering in. It was rushing in. In my flute-based joy I'd forgotten about the treacherous tides round here; the lifeguard gestured to us to climb on to the jeep and we all did and he whizzed across the sand. 'Don't do that again!' he shouted and, despite the turbulent journey, Snake played a riff that got us safely back to the path along the seafront. The lifeguard drove away, waving to us. Snake played him a farewell melody and we all went to the Ocean Fish Bar for haddock and chips.

It felt like a dream then, and it still feels like a dream. I'm sure it happened, though. Well, fairly sure. What do you think, Snake?

JAZZ AND BELLS AND EARLY
MORNING COFFEE

As teenagers, my mate Dave Sunderland and I were obsessed by jazz and bellringing. We'd meet up at his house on Friday evenings when his mam was out playing the organ at the chapel and listen to jazz on a fading station on his radio; in my memory it's an obscure Russian station but it may well have been Radio 2. We'd snap our fingers and pretend to be sophisticated as the music came and went. He liked Oscar Peterson and I liked Charlie Parker but we both liked The Peddlers, a Manchester-based jazz-rock trio that Les Dawson described as 'the last of the cheap bands' but we honestly didn't care. They swung like the clappers.

Ah, the clappers. Dave and I were also bellringers, practising each Thursday evening on Darfield's glorious ring of six bells, ringing those same bells each Sunday as well as ringing at a number of the area's smaller churches with just three bells. Three-bell ringing was unfashionable because, frankly, there's not much you can do with them. You can 1-2-3 or 2-1-3 or 3-1-2 or 2-1-3 or 3-2-1 or or 2-3-1 or 3-1-2 or 1-3-2 or or 3-2-1 and that's about it. It's like, as I commented to Dave one Friday night, listening to a jazz trio who have never learned to improvise.

Each year the Darfield Bellringers, under the leadership of the tower captain Mike King, went on a weekend junket to try ringing at other towers and one year in the mid-1970s we trekked in various cars and a minibus to the East Coast, to ring the bells in Scarborough and Whitby and one or two of the smaller churches nearby. We stayed in a place at the top of the festival of steepness that is Robin Hood's Bay and, really, because we were teenagers, the weekend was just an excuse to stay up late and talk bollocks. Dave Sunderland was and is an aficionado of the Yorkshire Coast and Scarborough is his favourite resort and he regaled us with tales of its history and architecture.

Late on the Saturday, as the night turned into the early morning in his room in that Robin Hood's Bay hotel that smelled of dust and fading summer dreams, we decided, on a whim, to drive to Scarborough to see the dawn. Dave had recently passed his test and was a careful but solid driver and so I had no qualms about entrusting my chubby frame to his gear-changing and emergency-stopping abilities.

Before we went, we charged the forthcoming trip with epic possibilities: the dawn would be the best one ever seen in the history of the world, or the history of Yorkshire, which is more or less the same thing. The Grand Hotel, that cathedral on the cliff, would have a coffee shop that was open to non-residents (see the specificity of our fantasy?) and would serve us espressos. Neither of us had ever had espressos of course; they didn't arrive in Barnsley until the Aroma Café in The Arcade started selling them in the mid-1990s, but we knew that hep cats drank them. Or rather sipped them. The other branch line of our fantasy was that there would be a jazz band still, miraculously, playing in the ballroom of the hotel. They would be playing to themselves because the guests had trickled to bed but they would see us and invite us in. They would play Oscar Peterson and Charlie Parker and we would order another espresso.

The night was giving up its ghosts as we drove down to Scarborough, Gerry Mulligan on the cassette player in Dave's car. Dawn was lighting a one-bar electric fire over the sea. We arrived in town like outriders of a conquering army; a cool conquering jazz army, to be precise. I wished I'd had the courage to buy and wear a pork-pie hat. There was nobody around because the last club had rolled the last guests out. The Grand Hotel dominated the skyline, like it always did and it always will. There were no lights on but that didn't bother us because we knew, thanks to a failed light bulb at Dave's house one evening, that jazz is best experienced in the dark.

We drove up and down the front, pretending that we were taking in the growing light but actually plucking up courage to go to the imposing doors of The Grand and ask to be admitted. Or jazz-admitted, because we both liked to play the language game of putting the word 'jazz' in front of any word to make it sound more sophisticated. After all, decades later, it would work with apples. Well, more or less. More or jazz less.

Eventually we stopped the jazz car, got out and walked towards the jazz door of the The Jazz Grand. I promise I'll stop doing that now. Stop jazz doing that now. There were lights on in the foyer. There was an imposing bell to ring. A mezzo-soprano gull mocked our hesitation so one of us rang the bell. It echoed somewhere in the hotel's soul. Nothing happened. Nothing happened again.

The sky blushed and light grew in confidence. A middle-aged man in a white shirt and bow tie shambled to the door. He was the gatekeeper to an early morning of choruses and solos; he was the barista who would make espressos that would keep us awake until the 1980s.

He mouthed the word 'closed'. He pointed to where a watch would have been on his wrist if he'd had a watch. Maybe he'd forgotten to put it on. Then his face softened a little, as though it was melting. 'Are you residents?' he mouthed. We shook our heads.

'We want jazz!' I shouted, too loud for the gull, which wheeled away. 'We want espressos and we want jazz!' He shook his head although to this day I think there was a twinkle in his eye that told me that he too wanted espressos and jazz in his life.

We walked away and strolled on the beach; the sun came up glowing like bell metal and Dave and I toasted each other with invisible cups. 'It don't mean a thing if it ain't got that espresso' Dave said, and we laughed.

JOE'S PRIZE BINGO AND THE LOCKOUT

Whenever my wife and I are travelling by train on the wonderful East Coast Main Line to Edinburgh, we start to feel a moment of excitement as we approach Berwick; this isn't just because we love that old Janus-faced straddler of a town, but because we know if Berwick is in the middle distance then Spittal is just ahead and we'll soon be seeing Joe's Prize Bingo. If we're lucky, the sun will be mining gold from the deep seams of the water. If we're really lucky the trolley will just have gone by and we'll be able to toast Joe's Prize Bingo with a cup of tea.

Every family has a portfolio of sacred sites, places that probably mean nothing to anybody else but to the people involved are as important as the attractions that get recommended in tourist guides. These locations, which are often unglamorous points in the folds in a map, get talked about at get-togethers, and during the pandemic and the lockdowns it was places like Joe's that we promised we'd go back to 'when it's all over' to sweat on the bottom line before we got a full house. JPB was (the building's still there, but it's not Joe's any more, which is a bit like renaming the Eiffel Tower, as far as I'm concerned) an unassuming place hunched by the North Sea, the sea that never forgets and never forgives. To us it's a combination of art gallery and theatre and dreamcatcher.

So that is why, as the train slows down towards Berwick, we stand and gaze at Joe's, and the time machine that squats in all our hearts whizzes us straight back to that summer in the early 1990s when Joe's really was the place to be. Well, for us it was.

We decided on Spittal on a whim, I think, that summer; we'd been to Berwick a few times and liked it, but we settled on a cottage in Spittal just a couple of hundred yards from the beach. If I examine my reasons for wanting to book that cottage, though, the glory of saying the word 'Spittal' out loud would come near the top of the list; my dad, a genial and gentle Scotsman, would love to say the phrase 'the Spittal of Glenshee' over and over again when he was planning an itinerary around The Auld Country. The Spittal of Glenshee is a tiny village in the Highlands not too far from Perth but he would repeat the phrase as often as he could even if we were only planning a trip to Jedburgh. He would sometimes say it in tandem with his other favourite place, 'the Ballachulish Ferry', and when put together it sounded like he was about to give us a lost Andy Stewart song. Maybe the pull that places have on us is to do with language as much as space; perhaps the names we give them are their not-so-secret portals. Spittal. Spittal. Spittal. Like father, like son.

The cottage was a huge stone-built edifice that faced the sea's whims and arguments with the kind of solidity you associate with a bloke propping up the bar at a country pub; in other words, solidity with a pocketful of stories. We unpacked and then walked down to the sea and the kids paddled; out on the horizon's hinterland rain grew in confidence but we didn't notice because, hey, we were all so much younger then.

The rain arrived at our party and sent us scuttling into the waiting arms of Joe's Prize Bingo. 'Eyes down for a full house' somebody, perhaps Joe himself, said. We obeyed and took our seats or rather took our high stools (the smaller kids being helped on) and listened as the numbers were read out. Any bingo game is a kind of performance and this was no exception; there weren't any histrionics or proto-rap rhythms here, however. It was a bit like listening to a calculator sing. It was like Samuel Beckett had written a play set in a seaside bingo hall. I found it gorgeous, and hypnotic, and beautiful like the sound of bicycle tyres in rain. We enjoyed shouting 'House!' too, and we were amused when a posh family sat near us and shouted 'Bingo!'

And of course we won things. Tiny plastic trinkets that shone like jewels. Toys that were so fragile they broke before you got them back to the cottage. Things that glowed and things that made tiny music. So Joe's Prize Bingo became our go-to place that holiday, and although we can't have gone there twice a day it feels in my memory that we went there twice a day. We didn't go ironically either; we weren't hipsters slumming it or arty types dipping our high toes in low culture. We loved it.

And then one day, towards the end of the holiday, we locked ourselves out of the cottage; I can't remember exactly how it happened, although it was probably my fault. One moment we could get into the cottage and the next minute we couldn't, like Adam and Eve and the kids being barred from Eden. These were the days before mobile phones, of course, so I couldn't ring the owner and anyway I didn't know their number. I went to a garage; I'm not sure why, because the cottage wasn't on wheels and didn't have an engine. The man looked at me with pity and then said he'd come and have a look later when he'd closed up but maybe the best bet would be if we smashed a window and then reached in and got the key, which we by now had determined was on the kitchen worktop.

And then we did a beautiful thing because there was nothing else to do; we went to Joe's Prize Bingo and got a couple of full houses and some winnings and we walked back to the cottage in the afternoon sun and somehow I knew that everything would be OK.

And it was. We all stood looking at the door as I tried to open it through the power of my mind. The man next door was in his yard, watering some tubs of plants. 'Are you locked out?' he asked. I nodded. 'It happens all the time,' he said. 'I've got a spare one', and he passed it to me and we got in.

And we were winners. And we had a Full House. And that is why I stand up to salute Joe's Prize Bingo every time I pass.

EAST COAST, MAGNETIC COAST

The end of a childhood holiday. The cases packed with almost as much sand as clothing. The sticks of rock for neighbours and mates, rattling in the car boot like artistic representations of rhubarb or celery. The bruise on the knee; there's always a bruise somewhere from a childhood holiday. The wistful glance at the sea, glancing back, mirrored.

And once, in the early 1960s, the sudden change of mind. My mother and dad and me and my brother had been for a week in Bridlington. I'd bought a toy robot that shuffled along and my knee-bruise was from a sudden trip on a side street looking for a comic shop we all had a vague memory of but never found. We were about to get in the car when my dad, for reasons I can never explain, decided that we could stay another two days. This was a quieter era before smartphones of course, so he couldn't have got a message from the office saying he wasn't needed for a while.

Somehow, I decided years later, he must have known beforehand that we could stay longer but had been undecided about staying on until the last minute. The forecast must have been good, or maybe the prospect of the office was bad.

We all sat in the car, unsure of what to do next. We'd emptied the caravan we'd rented and tidied it up and we were just about to go to the office and hand in the key. My dad said, 'I'll just ask if we can stay a bit longer. I'm sure it'll be fine.'

We drove to the office. The morning sun shone with uncomplicated promise. The bruise on my knee seemed to be fading. My dad went into the office and seemed to be gone a long time, long enough for the bruise to fade even more. My mother looked at her face in the vanity mirror on the sunshield and added more lipstick. My brother stared into the North Yorkshire air.

My dad came out of the office looking disappointed but hopeful, which is perhaps a look we should all carry throughout our lives. 'We can't go back to that caravan, it's booked out to a family from Kidderminster,' he said. I don't know why he or any of us thought the Kidderminster detail was important, but we did. 'But the man says we can have another caravan. I've got the key here.' He held up the key and it shone in the sun. I bet the Kidderminster Usurpers didn't have a shiny key. 'He says it's a bit small but we'll all fit in no bother.'

The caravan was at the edge of the field and it looked like a toy one or one that you might use in the reconstruction of a crime scene. 'Small' seems too long a word to describe the caravan; the key was almost bigger than the door.

My dad opened the door and the caravan interior did the opposite of looming. Renaissance artists living in this caravan would have had difficulty portraying perspective or light as it appeared to have neither. 'It'll be fine,' my dad said breezily, as he squeezed through the door like a giant in an animated film. We followed him in and stood very close to each other in the kitchenette which was more of a kitchenetteette. We were so close we were almost standing behind each other even though we were standing beside each other. We went into the living area and my dad pointed out a bed that seemed to be crouching in the corner of the ceiling like a spider. 'That'll be where you sleep,' my dad said. He pointed to a narrow strip of fabric under a window. 'That's a settee and it can also be your bed,' he said to my brother, who looked unimpressed. 'We'll go in here,' he went on, opening the door to a bedroom from a doll's house.

My dad thought it would be OK. My brother said he wished he'd brought a cat to see if he could swing it. My mother wasn't sure. I climbed into the bed and although it was a really tight squeeze because I was a fat lad (what my mother called 'stiffish'), I quite liked it. Earlier in the summer, goaded on by my mates Keith and Geoff, I'd managed to climb into a rabbit hutch and tell the lads it was quite comfortable in there. At least, it was until they locked the door and went home to watch *Fireball XL5* and I started to blubber and my mother had to come and liberate me. This bed felt a bit like that but without the lock and the tiny cannonballs of rabbit poo.

'It's too small,' my mother said, really just articulating what the rest of us knew all along. Half of me, at least half of me, wanted to stay. My brother looked relieved, or he would have done if there'd been enough space in the caravan to arrange his features into a relieved look.

My dad said he'd take the key back and we trudged to the car. The holiday was really over now. I started to cry because I felt that, with a bit of give and take and a lot of breathing in, we could have managed.

My dad disappeared into the camp office and, again, was gone for quite a long time. I sobbed quietly. My dad reached into his pocket and flourished a magnet, one of those traditional magnet-shaped ones, and gave it to me. 'I know you wanted to stay but here's a magnet from the camp shop,' he said. An unusual but effective sentence as it stopped my crying. All the way home I kept using the magnet to pick up a paper clip that my dad had found in his pocket. 'Little things please little minds,' my brother said. He was right.

Years later I visited Kidderminster and was convinced that some of the people I passed must have been the family that took our caravan. I wished I'd got a magnet to pull the buttons off their coats and the grips out of their hair. Some bruises never fade.

WHO'S THAT IN THE PICTURE?

Yes, but who is that in the picture? Who is that lurking in the album, hanging around at the edge of the slide, checking for messages on the borders of a Facebook film? Who's that young lad/young man/middle-aged man/older man with the brown hair/grey hair/white hair? It's me, of course, Ian McMillan, not only the star of my own life but also a bit-part player, an extra, an unpaid intern sneaking into your life with a daft grin and an upthumb. Or a vacant look. Or with a gobful of chips.

Of course everybody is on a photograph now, wherever they are and whatever time it is, but the seaside picture is a particularly honest form of the genre because it's here, I reckon, that we're at our most unbuttoned. We're spectacularly informal and, probably more than at any other time in our lives, we don't mind being photographed. 'Just let me get my comb-over straight first; oh, never mind, it's too windy. Just take the bloody picture!' I guess the exceptions to this rule are the Instagram Influencers who have to make sure that their pecs are lined up symmetrically and their cheekbones are sharpened and their buttocks are contoured perfectly before they can allow themselves to be lifted into the world's gaze but let's face it, they're not like the rest of us, the ones with red sauce on our white shirts, the ones with a dog jumping up at them just at the moment the shutter clicks, the ones who haven't closed their eyes all day but close them at the exact moment of the photograph. We are the ones who want photographic evidence that we were at the seaside so that we can look at it when we're locked down or locked up or locked into a stopped train.

Perhaps there's a deep history to this. When I was a child all our photograph albums, and we had many of them, were crowded with variations of the same snap: a family or a couple walking down a seafront or on a promenade or along a beach. The grins are wide and the clothes are natty and the attitude certainly isn't that of Stalin at Yalta or a celebrity caught out without make-up. The thing that intrigued me as a lad was that on these pictures everybody was there: the mam, the dad, the kids. So who took the photo? A passing stranger? Well, I now know it was usually the work of professional beach photographers from the days when few people could afford a camera. These chaps (usually chaps) would accost you as you strolled and get you to pose and then you'd go and collect the finished prints at the end of the pier just before your trip bus or the excursion train went back.

I think I caught the very tail end of this tradition because I have a vivid memory of being about four or five years old, walking down the seafront at somewhere that may have been Colwyn Bay, and a man in a dark suit like the ones insurance men used to wear said in what I recall as a very high-pitched voice 'Watch the birdie, folks, watch the birdie' and I looked but there was no bird. My dad shook his head and the man's camera clicked and he gave my dad a card and said 'By the station front at half past five' and my mother said 'Do you think we should?' and my dad, always a stickler for honesty, said 'No, we don't have to.' He might even have said 'We haven't entered into a legally binding contract' but I think as I got older I must have reimagined and re-remembered that section of the day.

Then, as the camera became an essential adjunct to the holiday for families who could afford them, the beach photographer disappeared and we were all put in charge of our own presents and pasts. I'm very interested, however, in the way that I have ended up on other people's pictures.

Here I am, lounging by a wall in the wonderfully named Eyemouth near Berwick-upon-Tweed; it's a harbour with a soul and a sky that seems freshly painted every day. I'm lounging by the wall and somebody is taking a picture of the harbour and there I am in the frame. When they look at that picture they will wonder why I'm frowning; I'm frowning because a council cleaner in a hi-vis jacket is scooping up a more or less dead gull and putting it into a black sack. I know: that would make you frown too.

Here I am at Seahouses in Northumberland; I'm about to take a lick of a huge ice cream and the heat suddenly wins its battle against the cold and a huge berg of ice cream follows the rules of gravity all over my chin and because I'm on holiday I don't care and I'm happy to sport an ice-cream goatee. The camera clicks and I'm captured in a stranger's history.

Here I am in Aldeburgh in Suffolk. I'm having a good time but it's mid-afternoon and because I wake up so early this is the time of day I start to slump like a half-inflated balloon. I start to yawn and the yawn grows and grows until I am like an opera singer with the sound down. I could be a man who has gone to a fancy-dress party as the mouth of a cave. A couple who are very much in love ask someone else to take their picture and it's just as they stand with their arms around each other that my yawn reaches its climax. I guess I'll get a laugh at their silver wedding anniversary party when the picture is blown up to ten times its original size and displayed on the wall of the village hall where the event is happening. Of course they might have got divorced and the yawn might take on terrible significance but I hope that doesn't happen.

And maybe, just maybe, they were the same people who took each photograph. Eyemouth, Seahouses, Aldeburgh, not following me around but just briefly occupying the same coastal space on the map so that their memories include The Frowning Man, The Ice Cream Man, The Yawning Man. Ah well, it's a kind of fame.

MY SAND LIFE, MY PEBBLE LIFE

My sand life, my pebble life. My deckchair failure life in that stiff breeze. My eyes filling with tears life as I gaze at a far horizon and think of the people I will never play on this beach with; a ferry passes, going somewhere. My shorts life, the blown beach jabbing me with tiny injections. My listening life, the shell to my ear hoping for the sea and getting myself hissing back. My horizon life, imagining my dad always looking for a new one, always finding a new one. My language life, trying to wrestle these things into words as a gull laughs and a roundabout spins and spins, the mouths of the horses wide open.

My sand life, my pebble life. My life as a series of temporary sandcastles waiting for the tide to throw them in its washing machine; or that lolly stick I used as a flagpole that will soon be swept away. O, my life of embarrassment in front of those others, finding a teabag in the sea and telling people I'd found a sea urchin and it was obvious I didn't know what a sea urchin was. O, my listening life: at the edge of the crowd listening to a beach preacher preach hell and damnation and thinking that the black clouds gathering around the lighthouse were judgement on my ice cream, my frivolous ice cream. My pork-pie life; so happy I could burst in a hand-knitted jumper eating the crust first so as not to spoil the delayed gratification.

My sand life, my pebble life. My donkey life: I am so high up I think I am flying; someone asks me to wave for a camera and as I wave I realise that gravity is winning and that the ground is miles away. My torch life on a late-night beach where me and the others look like mobile constellations looking for the sky. My postcard-writing life; what else can I say? Can I say nothing and still say something? Can I say something and still say nothing? How do I finish? Where do I finish? Why is the address so long and the stamp so big?

My sand life, my pebble life. My running and screaming life as my brother fishes a spider crab from a rock pool and chases me with it, waving it like a leggy mop, whooping a strange whoop; the spider crab seems to have at least twenty limbs and each one of them wants to scratch me and worse, take me back to the pool which is not like the pool with the crabs in The Perishers that I read in the *Daily Mirror* earlier. My lost hat life; my running after the hat like the boy ran after the gingerbread man in the story I read to my children and still read to my grandchildren; the tide is out but let's face it the tide will be in by the time I've caught this hat.

My sand life, my pebble life. My life getting my trunks back on under a towel when I've tentatively dipped a couple of areas of myself into the fridgy sea and the wind threatens to Marilyn Monroe my towel just as the trunks are off and the pants are almost off. My sunset life, holding up a camera to try to capture some kind of special moment but waiting too long, far too long, hoping for a kind of spectral purple or a lone bird making a silhouette across the frame; too long, too long, the sun's curtain is down. My bucket and spade life and the spade can never be big enough to dig to Australia with and the bucket can never be big enough to hold all the sand but I'll keep digging even though Uncle Jack said Australia isn't straight down China's straight down but I'll keep digging I'll keep digging.

My sand life, my pebble life. My life of sand all across the bedroom floor even though I've been home for a couple of days;

the beach has become a kind of mobile library that brings me stories wherever I go. My pebble life; that constellation of rocks on the shelf, each one from a particular beach but because I haven't labelled them I don't know which but that doesn't stop them being beautiful just as trees are still sublime even if you don't know the name of the tree. My flask life; this is a piece of mime that I could take to the Edinburgh Fringe and play to packed houses with because the flask lid has never been this tight before or I have never been this weak before and is my grimace helping? Maybe not.

My sand life, my pebble life. My life measured out in tides, coming in and going out and doing the same again. My life measured out in games of trying to spot the sea first. My life measured out in the delicious and indulgent sadness that comes from leaving a holiday cottage for the last time and for the first time in several days it isn't raining but at least the kids have had a great time and, let's face it, so have you.

My sand life, my pebble life.

FILEY FACT, FILEY FICTION

For many years I planned to write a short story about this; a story that would be published by a mainstream literary outlet like *The London Magazine*. The story would get a little bit of attention and a publisher would contact me to see if I could write a whole collection of stories in a similar vein and I would write loads of them and achieve a kind of short story fame which is like real fame but shorter and sometimes with a twist in the tale and sometimes with a kind of modernist dying fall.

The trouble was, I never wrote the story. I planned it a lot and may have even got a couple of paragraphs down but I never took the plunge into the body of the tale. It was like the story was a zebra crossing on a busy road that I daren't step on to. Maybe the trouble was that nothing much happened, and the little bits that did happen only made (and continue to make) profound sense to me. And then not always. That shouldn't stop something being a successful story, of course, but I wanted resonance and I wanted transcendence and I couldn't locate either of them anywhere no matter how hard I looked.

We were on holiday in Filey, on the East Coast, and the kids were small. We stayed in a little guest house a short walk up a steep hill from the beach. It was a glorious summer and we spent all day on those fabulous sands building sandcastles and memories and knocking them down. That's the sandcastles not the memories.

One day something got spilt on our travelling rug, as it often did, and my wife asked me if I would go back to the guest house to get some wipes, which we'd left on the old-fashioned sideboard in the room, which had a mysterious A to Z of Birmingham in one of the drawers.

There was something almost elegiac about going into the guest house in the late morning. The place was empty; the cleaners had gone and I saw the owner and his wife walking down the road carrying shopping bags. We nodded, although I knew that they had no real idea who they were nodding to in a life built on brief encounters and egg preferences. I guess we were all just so many rumpled pillows and Jackson Pollock plates.

I let myself into the room and stood in the quiet space that was like a Museum of Daydreaming. Somewhere in the unimagined distance a radio played classical music. I picked up the wipes and wandered back to the beach. To the noise and the bustle of the beach. I splashed in the sea with the kids; I built sandcastles and knocked them down. I ate a sandwich and ran up and down. The tide turned slowly but couldn't be bothered to advance. My elder daughter was a little upset because she'd left her magazine in the room. I volunteered to go and get it, partly to cheer her up but also because I wanted, I really wanted, to go back to the cathedral-like quality of that little cube with the dressing table and the beds and the TV that was as big as an envelope.

I walked back up and let myself in. A squirrel watched me from a tree. That classical music still played somewhere, or nowhere. I stood in the room again, clutching the magazine's brightness. I sat down on the bed. I wasn't tired because I was young but I felt that if I just closed my eyes for a minute I might be able to become part of the music; a violin solo, maybe. Or perhaps that charged silence between movements that are a taut chasm of unclapping. I closed my eyes. Somehow I felt that I could hear my children shouting for me. Of course there were no mobile phones in those days or I would have got an emoji-festooned text or WhatsApp message. Instead I stood up, picked up the magazine and walked down the narrow lighthouse-like stairs to the open air. The owners were back; they nodded at me again and I said 'Kate forgot her *Shout*', which would have made no sense to them but they smiled. My face was reflected in the glass of a painting of Filey that I passed on the way out. That moment would have been the crux of the story I was going to write, the one I never wrote. There was something about me being reflected in the place I was about to walk down to that seemed significant.

I walked back to the beach. The kids had a donkey ride and Kate read her magazine. We had an ice cream and I spilled a bit down my top but nobody cared. I had a camera but, given the shape of the story I never got round to writing, I had left it in the room. I said to my wife that I was going to go and get the camera to take a couple of photos before the sun went home.

For the third time, like the cockerel in the pre-Crucifixion story, I went back to the guest house. I let myself in. There was a scent of polish and ghost-breakfasts. A Filey-light hung in the wide hall, floating with dust motes. The visitors' book reminded me that when we left I would have to sign it and the kids would too. Maybe that would be another crux, later in the story.

I left the guest house. I walked back to the beach and took photographs in the golden hour. As I said, nothing happened. So why, as I write this, am I feeling huge waves of emotion wash over me? Why do I wish that I could go back to that guest house and stand there as though I have just stepped out of the wallpaper?

THE SHAPE OF THE WATCH
ON THE WRIST

A woman looms towards us, silhouetted in the blazing sun so that she looks like a cardboard cut-out of herself. Because my head is aching and spinning just a little, she looks like a cardboard cut-out of herself as done by a child. She points at us and says 'You're going to be so burned in the morning.' She walks away. She comes back, a returning silhouette, and says 'So, so burned.' She walks away again. My head feels like somebody is playing lacrosse with it. Somebody who has never played lacrosse before and has no idea of the rules. I wish the sun would get turned off with an audible click.

I've never sunbathed before; some people love it and it's their idea of a holiday but I prefer a nice cool art gallery, perhaps with abstracts called *The Sunbathers* that I can make jokes about along the lines of 'Well, he should have put more sun cream on' as I point to a splash and a line. My wife and I and her sister and her husband are on holiday in the USA. We've been to New York and we've driven in a hire car the size of a furniture shop up to New England and we're staying in a motel near a beach. I can't remember the name of the motel or the beach but because I very rarely get headaches I can recall the shape and whirring machine of the headache. It's the shape of Benbecula and it whirs like a third hand hair dryer.

All these decades later, I can't recall why we all decided to sunbathe, given that none of us were sun worshippers. Maybe we had had enough of sightseeing and wanted to make sights of ourselves; maybe the extreme heat and burning orb in the sky made us lethargic. Maybe (we were young then) we thought that's what young people should do. We found a quiet area of the beach and lay down on towels. We were, I'm ashamed to say, desultory about sun cream in a way that we wouldn't have been today. We threw a bit on. We rubbed half-heartedly. The sun grinned and started to cook us.

We stayed where we were all day except for trips to stalls to buy ice cream and hot dogs. That's two separate trips. At the ice-cream stall the man listened as I placed my order and asked 'What part of New Zealand are you from? I love New Zealand!' I told him I was from Barnsley but I could tell he didn't believe me. 'Hope you guys have got plenty of cream,' he said, 'I know you don't get a lot of sun in New Zealand.' I wandered off. 'Hey, Kiwi!' he shouted. 'I meant sun cream not ice cream!' His laugh was as brittle as toffee that was too hard to be chewed.

It was hard, because we'd never done this sunbathing thing before, to decide when we'd had enough. I, for one, felt slightly uncomfortable but maybe that's how sunbathing always was; maybe the reason people lay prone without moving was that they were in too much filigreed agony to move. In the end, we let the sun decide for us as it began to fall into the sea. I looked around. We were the only ones left on the sand. I glanced at my watch; I hardly ever wear watches but I'd taken one on this holiday for reasons that remain obscure to me. It was 6pm and it felt like we'd been horizontal for ever apart from hot dog and ice cream verticalisms. We decided to go back to the motel and then go out somewhere to eat gigantic steaks and enormous bits of cheesecake.

Before we went out, though, we'd sit down for a minute, just have a minute like the old people we would one day become, having struggled up a long hill. Just for a minute. The room was whirling and somehow moving up and down at the same time, as though we were taking part in a psychedelic earthquake session. We all lay down on the various hard beds. I held on to my bed to stop it trying to walk away but that just seemed to make it angry.

I felt simultaneously hot and cold, like The Great Fire of London and The Great Freeze of 1948 were happening at once in this motel room with its Bronze Age air conditioning that sounded like a Frank Zappa out-take. One of us, or maybe all of us, said 'I think we've been out in the sun too long.' The sentence hit us like a hard brick of fact. We had a kind of sunstroke, I reckon. We were Yorkshire cats and the sun had stroked us. I stood up and took my watch off because in my fried state I thought that if I didn't know what time it was I might feel a bit cooler.

I took my watch off but my watch was still on; my skin had reddened around where the watch had been and so I was wearing a ghost watch that was probably still telling me the time from before I lay down on the beach's hotplate. I felt a laugh bubbling up from somewhere. I opened my mouth and the laugh fell out, followed by another and another. I shook like somebody miming an earthquake. The others saw me and they started laughing too. Soon we were laughing so much that none of us could breathe; we were still terribly, terribly hot and the laughter was at the tremulous edge of laughter where it elides into counterfeit pain and then into real pain. The laughter subsided until I said the words 'New Zealand' and then it began again. It subsided again. I held up my arm with the invisible watch and the laughter began again. It subsided again until I said the words 'So, so burned'.

Listen: you can still hear it above the sound of the waves.

THE MAP OF GETTING THE MAP

One of my dad's great joys when we went on our holidays to the coast in the 1960s was to send off for a route map from the AA. This was in the days when, as far as our family was concerned, the AA was as much a vital part of the social fabric as the BBC or the NHS. It was the days when people still saluted the AA man as he drove by on his motorbike.

The route map would arrive a few weeks before the trip and my dad would spend ages planning the trip with the AA map open on the table next to at least one atlas and maybe an Ordnance Survey map or two so that he looked like he was plotting a military operation. I guess in some ways he was, because he had been in the Royal Navy for many years and had served in the Second World War. In 1965 we were only twenty years after the ceasefire and the conflict loomed hugely in everybody's cultural and political imagination even if, like me (because I was only nine in 1965) we weren't able to articulate it in that way.

From the vantage point of the locked-down and Zooming spring of 2021, my dad sending off for what was in effect a paper satnav seems prehistorically quaint. The year in question we booked the first of our many holidays at the Tan-y-Marian Guest House in Llandudno and even the method of booking the break seems like something a dinosaur might have done. We had no telephone (I assume the Tan-y-Marian had one) so my dad wrote to the guest house asking if they had a room free on the dates in question. The guest house wrote back and said that they had. My dad wrote back and asked if he could book the room. The guest house wrote back and said that he could. My dad wrote back saying that he would like to book the room and asking if they would like a deposit paid by cheque or postal order. This went on for weeks and became a kind of epistolary novel that very few people would admit to wanting to read.

So for our family the sending and receiving of mail was an integral part of any holiday, it was the starting gun that the clicking of the letterbox fired. And we were off. Very slowly, in a blue Ford Zephyr with the registration number UHE 8.

At least two days before the holiday the AA route map would be positioned behind the clock on the mantelpiece in the front room next to the wall through which we could hear Mr Page next door practising the piano. Whenever I think of those yellow AA route maps, they always have a soundtrack of chapel hymns and that is why. 'Hills of the North, Rejoice' in particular.

Then, on the morning of the trip, once the car had been packed up and the picnic had been prepared and the stove had been tested, me or my brother John would be sent to fetch the route map and the holiday could start properly because as my dad once said, 'The holiday begins when you leave the house on the first day', which is something I've believed ever since.

Except on the day we went to the Tan-y-Marian the route map wasn't there. The clock was there, the mantelpiece was there. Mr Page's piano was there, altering the air. But the route map wasn't. I went to tell my dad and his normally cheerful and optimistic face fell. 'It must be there!' he said, his voice rising an octave and cracking like a dropped side plate. He went into the room to check for himself: clock, mantelpiece, Methodist hymn several choruses in. No route planner.

My brother had a bright idea, which seemed bright for about as long as he spoke then it burned out more or less as soon as it left his mouth and sat there smouldering. 'We could use the map book and I could navigate us,' he said with a teenager's confidence. My mother shook her head. 'You get car sick anyway,' she said, 'and that would make it worse.' It was true. Even a short trip to the shops made him bilious. The family method of controlling the sickness, which had something to do with a belief in the movement of static electricity from the car to the body, was for my brother to sit on a folded copy of the *Daily Mirror*, preferably on the page with the Donald Zec column on. It did seem to work intermittently, but only for about the first thirty miles. It was certainly the case that if he'd been following our journey across the country on the map and then glancing up at road signs, even Donald Zec couldn't help. Or Cassandra. Or Jane. My mother didn't fancy it; she was a nervous passenger anyway, often believing that the car was about to crash or at least develop three flat tyres simultaneously. I would have liked to have had a go but I was too young to be trusted. It was a huge and crushing problem because my dad always wanted to know where he was going and now he didn't know where he was going, or rather he knew where he was going but he had absolutely no idea how to get there.

He looked behind the clock again as though it was some kind of Tardis and the passage of time would somehow have made the map appear. It hadn't.

My dad was a practical person and not one to despair for very long. He took a roll of white paper out of the adding machine he sometimes brought home from the office and declared that he was going to recreate the route map for us. My mother put the kettle on and my brother folded up a couple of *Daily Mirror*s ready for the trip.

It's a picture of domestic harmony, so I won't disturb it by pointing out that later that day, just as we were about to set off, we found the route map in the glovebox of the car.

CARRYING THE METHODIST

Understand that all of the tale I'm about to tell is lit by light from the sea; at times this sea is distant, although it gets a little closer as the story progresses, but the light is bright and constant, winking from the water, unleashing a kind of bonsai searchlight into the hills where two men are carrying a woman.

I don't want to jump ahead of myself, though, so just think about the light, the light from the Welsh sea, as complex as a Dylan Thomas line, as simple as an RS Thomas image. Here we are on holiday somewhere in North Wales; there's me, and my mam and my dad and my brother John, and my mam's old school mate Mary and her husband Jack and her daughter Josephine. Yes, you're right; quite a crowd of us decanted from South Yorkshire in the mid-1960s in two cars that went so slowly they were sometimes overtaken by the seasons.

On the journey down to the caravan park we were staying in we'd tried out our new messaging system. These days 'messaging system' suggests something floating, hovering and landing in cyberspace. For us it meant a series of boards with letters painted on them; I think we'd got the idea from an item on *Blue Peter* or the local news. The idea was that if you wanted to get a message to the car you were travelling with you pulled up alongside and a passenger (not the driver, obviously, that would be silly) held up one of the signs. T meant 'it's time for a toilet break'. P didn't mean it was time for a toilet break but it meant

'Time for a picnic'. A question mark meant 'We are lost'. PE meant 'We need petrol'.

It might be just my overactive imagination bouncing off the curves of time but I seem to recall passing a number of cars with passengers holding up similarly lettered cardboard rectangles. It was like driving through an explosion in a Scrabble factory. I was in charge of the cards and I still flush with the embers of disappointed embarrassment when I remember holding the T one upside down. Uncle Jack teased me about it for years when he wasn't teasing me about the Barnsley FC score, him being a Sheffield Wednesday fan.

We spent a lot of time on the beach but then one day we drove a tiny way inland, a distance that felt like just a few yards because the sea still loomed huge in the back window of our blue Zephyr 6. My dad had read in the local newspaper about a hill that you could climb up an easy route to get a view of the sea and he proposed that we should all try it one day, taking a picnic with us. I remember that I had a new rucksack and, for reasons best known to myself, I folded the P sign into one of the vast (to a child) pockets. My plan was to flourish it just before our picnic started, to general hilarity.

If the jewelled and many-storied sea is a talisman for my memory of that day, then another emblem of it is a lovely watch that my mother was wearing; it had a dark blue rectangular face and the fingers and numbers were picked out in gold. If I had understood what the word 'sophisticated' meant, I would have described it as sophisticated.

We set off up the hill; it was more of an idea of a hill than a hill, except when you got near the top and the path suddenly narrowed and trees crowded in jostling your personal space, trying to spot what you'd got in your rucksack. The sun shone blamelessly as though it had no history at all and as though it had never seen terrible things. The folded P sign stuck uncomfortably into my back. We reached the top, and a flat picnic area; I waved the sign like a magician with a rabbit or, to be more precise, a trainee magician with a cardboard rabbit, and I got a few chuckles. Perhaps they were all tired after the climb. My mother sat down and, for some reason, loosened her watch strap.

Then a sudden kerfuffle caught our attention. Old men in shiny suits staggered towards us; their hair shone with oil and sweat and their suits had obviously been close friends for decades. At the front of the mass of suits, a couple of beefy older citizens were carrying a woman who winced with pain every time they took a step. It was a bit like the bit in those Frankenstein films I was sometimes allowed to stay up and watch when the mob ran through the streets with the body of the girl the monster had killed, although none of this fairly decorous mob looked like they would be running anywhere very soon. Or very fast.

The two woman-carriers looked relieved to see my dad and Uncle Jack and they stopped staggering and laid the woman gently down on the grass. I can still remember that she was wearing a hat and that the hat didn't move an inch as she met the earth, a fact that still amazes me.

One of the men tentatively approached my dad and spoke softly to him; I was standing close enough to tell that he was speaking Welsh. My dad shook his head emphatically and the man carried on in English, although I'm sure he would rather have been speaking Welsh.

My dad nodded, Uncle Jack nodded, and they both took the woman from the men and began to help her down the path to the bottom of the hill. It was a long, slow journey during which we learned that they were from a little chapel in the valley and they'd been on their annual pilgrimage to the top of the hill when Bronwen had slipped and twisted her ankle and, although the men were probably older than the hill they were walking up, they had to try to get her back down the hill. And that was when we turned up.

They were so grateful that they invited us back to their little chapel to eat sandwiches and drink tea and eat Welsh cakes, which we accepted; my overwhelming memory of that afternoon, though, is of my mother looking at her wrist and realising that her watch had fallen off somewhere on the path.

I bet it's still there, ticking its English tick.

THE WALLET

This is a story that fades and wriggles into and out of a dream state, a kind of fugue, a kind of flat country with unexpected hills that weren't there a moment ago but which are suddenly there, really and indisputably there. Until they're not. The story happens in the past and the present at the same time, like the pages of a diary flapping in a stiff breeze.

We're in Llandudno, one of our favourite coastal towns; me, my wife and our three children. Look more closely. In the evening light, if you look hard enough, it could be that we're a different family from many years before: my mam and dad and me and my brother because Llandudno was one of our special places then too. The ghosts of the people we were are walking just a little ahead of us and just a little behind us, occupying more or less the same space as us, like Velcroed shadows.

Me and my wife and the kids are just walking back to the guest house we're staying in and we're all tired; the sun and the wind have sucked the energy from us and I'm looking forward to the half-sleep I'll get tonight as the street lights and then the sun push their way through the undecided curtains.

We'd been in a café where a carton of Ribena my younger daughter had had was so out of date it should have been in a museum and when I pointed it out to the owner, a man who seemed to be at least half beard, he went into a back room and returned with a souvenir pencil, which he gave me by way of apology. Sometimes the pencil still turns up in a drawer and I think about that holiday.

As we make our steady way towards the Tan-y-Marian Guest House I notice something on the floor, something brown and leathery that could, from a distance, be a small tortoise or a dropped gauntlet. It's a wallet, the sort that could have been a constant and well-loved companion for its owner. Well, until it met the pavement.

I bent down and picked it up and my dad bent down too; he bent to pick up a different wallet at a different time in a different coastal town, Portree on the Isle of Skye. Yes, he is part shadow and part balaclava-made-of-midges because this is August in the Islands. And because he is in that place called The Past.

My dad briefly uses the found wallet as a midge-bludgeon but only succeeds in hitting his own face, which offers him a little relief and the rest of us a cheap chortle. I decide that, despite the fact we are all tired and craving sandy sleep, we should take the wallet to the police station; after all, as I reason to the rest of the party, if I lost my wallet and somebody found it I'd be very pleased if they handed it in. I ask a man where the police station is and from his pointing and detailed directions I decide that it's on the way back to the Tan-y-Marian. This, sadly, is not the case. The Cop Shop seems to be closer to my house in South Yorkshire than it is to the guest house's comforting smell.

We realise this as we walk round and round in the concentric circles I'm sure the man wasn't indicating with his broad-brushstroke hand gestures. In the past, my dad is clutching the wallet he's found as the sun goes down reluctantly and the gulls sing in Gaelic. A man approaches us; from the past's vast distance I can remember that the man has a black eye and a cut on his chin. He's drunk and swaying to invisible crooning music.

The kids are desperate to go to bed, but ahead of us, not too far away, I can see the police station. The wallet feels bulgy and I am living a kind of fantasy that it contains an old man's life savings and that he'll be so grateful for the return of his dosh that he'll give us a reward; not too much, but let's face it, the kids need new school shoes. We enter the police station; a man stands behind the desk and for a moment, because I'm tired and sun-bleached, I think he's a glove puppet.

Back on the Isle of Skye, the drunk and bloody man approaches my dad, points at the wallet and says something slurry and vowel-heavy. My dad shakes his head and puts the wallet in his pocket for safekeeping. The man stands and shouts at my dad, inches from his face, his breath enveloping us all, then he wanders off, exaggerating the motion of the earth. We walk towards the police station to hand the wallet in. I ask my dad what the man said to him and my dad replies 'He was asking for the train fare to Perth' and he and my mother exchange a loaded glance.

In Llandudno, I hand the wallet over to the cardboard cut-out copper and he moves. As I'm handing it over I remember my dad finding the wallet in Portree and I entertain a fantasy that maybe this is the same wallet, lost again and found again so that it becomes like one of those folk tales/urban myths about the man who lost his wedding ring in a deep lake and years later caught a trout in the same deep lake and when he cut it open to cook it there was the ring.

Suddenly my dad and I are signing forms in police stations far from home. Names and addresses are taken and we are thanked, a generation apart. The wallets are placed in evidence bags and two families, with me the only common conduit between time frames, trudge back to B&Bs.

And I never got a reward; not that I'd have wanted one, of course. Of course.

I HAVEN'T SEEN ONE OF THOSE
FOR YEARS

You'll have gathered as you make your way across this book's wide beach (sandals off, holding them in your hand as you wander) that I'm more of a wanderer than a sailor. Give me a cliffside path over a speedboat ride any day. Let me lounge in a harbourside café and let me not be tempted by a trip round the bay on a bobbing vessel.

As you'll also have seen from these pages, however, I did spend some time making a few little films for the TV programme *Coast*, which often involved something the producers called Mild Jeopardy and which at the time would often scare me to death but which would provide me with handy anecdote-fodder for years to come.

And I guess that's why I'm slithering around like an ungainly eel on the slippery floor of a cave not far from the seaside town of Girvan in Ayrshire. 'Take your time' the director says, holding a light. I should have been warned about the mild jeopardy in this shoot when the cameraman's business card, which fell from his bag as he hoisted it up, declared him to be not just a cameraman but an Adventure Cameraman.

In this bit of the film I was to scramble around in the cave to tell the story of Sawney Bean. Briefly, Sawney Bean was a Scottish cannibal in the eighteenth century who would lure unsuspecting travellers into his cave and eat them with much smacking of lips.

My dad used to say the name in a scary voice if he wanted to frighten me, but because he was so gentle and kind I just had to pretend to be scared, sometimes so convincingly that my dad apologised. The scrambly bit in the cave was the most difficult bit, the producer told me. The next day would be the easy day: I just had to interview somebody on the beach (Jeopardy: getting a pebble in my shoe) and then I had to do some pieces to camera from a boat as another smaller boat followed to film me gazing moodily out to sea when I'd finished talking to the camera (Jeopardy: slight headache from moody gazing). That night I slept well and in the morning I had a hearty breakfast just because I was in a hotel and also because talking to a camera and gazing moodily out to sea never counts as work to me. One day I will definitely get that badge that reads 'Will spout bollocks for cash'.

The first part of the filming, the interview on the beach, went well once both the interviewee and I had got used to the discomfort of sitting on pebbles and once she'd got used to the fact that I would be asking her the same questions over and over again and that she'd have to give more or less the same answers as the Adventure Cameraman caught us and preserved us from different angles. We all got used to looking at the sky as the sun went behind a cloud and somebody shouted 'Waiting for the light!' The camera lingered over shots of me and the interviewee wandering down the beach with the sea behind us, as flat as a picnic table.

Then it was time to get on the small boat and wait for the smaller boat to start to chug behind us as we headed out to sea. I did a couple of pieces to camera and a selection of Moody Gazes. The sea was calm and the breeze was more invigorating than intimidating. I stood by the man who was steering the boat and we chatted and the cameraman filmed it; he filmed it in an adventurous way by climbing on top of the fragile-looking cabin to capture the tops of our heads.

Then the captain (I reckon that's what he was) pointed out to sea where the horizon was a smudge, a line of faint paint spilt on a distant kitchen floor. 'I've not seen one of those for years,' he said conversationally. 'One of what?' I said. I imagined he might be pointing out an albatross. 'A wave like that,' he said. 'It might get a bit lumpy.'

Ah, the good old English language telling you exactly what was going to happen but then curling it around metaphor's little finger. The last time I'd heard 'lumpy' used in this context was as I sat on a tiny plane as it trundled down the runway at the short-lived Sheffield City Airport at the start of a flight to Belfast. Strong winds whipped over the motorway by the Tinsley Viaduct and the plane jostled and jolted alarmingly. And we were still on the tarmac. The air hostess came round with a basket of mints. The pilot's voice crackled over the tannoy: 'Ladies and gentlemen, as you can see it's a touch windy so the ascent will be a little lumpy.'

He was right. As the plane struggled to climb the sky's scaffolding, the man behind me said 'I wish I'd gone on the boat!' I sucked my mint.

And now here it was again. The L word. The wave rushed towards us as though it was pleased to see us. It slapped the boat like we were a fly and it was a swatter. We roller-coastered around and my hearty breakfast planned hearty revenge. The small boat behind us was being hurled about even more than we were. The man steering it was laughing. He was shouting something to me but I couldn't hear him; I cupped my ear and staggered to the back of the boat. His mouth was open like the cave we'd been filming in the day before. He had a very loud voice and eventually I caught what he said in my cupped ear. 'I WENT TO BARNSLEY ONCE,' he said. I raised a feeble thumb.

We tried to do my pieces to camera, we really tried. It wasn't too bad for me because I had something to concentrate on but the boat was lurching around so much that the lurching was taking over the story so that my pieces to camera became less about Sawney Bean and more about the weather conditions. To my relief the decision was taken to turn back and do the pieces to camera walking around the walls of Girvan Harbour which, as far as we knew, would stay very solid and still. 'Right, we're turning back,' the director said. I tried to sound casual when I asked the captain how long it would take. I pointed to the safe haven of Girvan Harbour, which looked as though it was just at the far end of a fairly long room.

'About two and a half hours,' he said. There is a word for the way time can stretch into something impossibly and tortuously long: lumpy.

GOING TO EXTREMES: NORTH

The sandals and the socks against the tide,
The Simmer Dim as hesitating light,
This morning holding hands with late last night.
Life's first long draft, with later drafts implied:
The beach invites the waves out for a ride.
My sandals and my socks give up the fight,
Succumb to dampness. Grinning with delight
I squelch across The Great Northern Outside.
This slice of year pushes horizons back
Until they touch each other in the sky
In pencil lines across an empty sheet;
Midsummer hands me something that I lack:
As sense of movement, seabirds wheeling by.
The day has turned. Now time to dry my feet.

GOING TO EXTREMES: EAST

Right here is where the brand new day begins
Where blue takes over, painted on the map,
A portrait of an edge, a line, a flap
A moment in the bright world as it spins.
Fresh paleness spreads across the eastern sky
I run towards the blank page of the sea
To write across it, splash out 'This is me!'
Beneath the morning sun's unblinking eye.
East is always sunrise, always growing
Along a coast that's reborn every time
The sky a stained-glass window in the sun
Until the high tide says 'I must be going'
And turns and ebbs away like a lost rhyme.
The poem has ended. Dawn's clean colours run.

GOING TO EXTREMES: WEST

This place is where the setting sun sets fire
To all the endless wide expanse of sea.
Here at the land's far edge I find the wire
Connecting us all loosely. Look at me
Silent and gazing within and without
To find the meaning that the coast implies;
Places like this can edge the mind with doubt.
Across the air a lonely lost cloud flies
Towards the sunset's moment in the glow
That is its soul, reminding me that here
Something's extinguished. As I turn to go
A window's wiped, a future is made clear:
Each sunset's just a sunrise's first draft
And we're all sailing home in time's long craft.

GOING TO EXTREMES: SOUTH

I used to think that *South* was all downhill,
That if you trickled down the map you'd find
A point where land would simply pause, then spill
Into a southern seascape of the mind.
A distant ship gives perspective; my eye
Is drawn towards its floating geometry.
This gentle wind is no more than a sigh
And sky and water touch in symmetry,
On days like this they settle and align.
I walk towards the waves across the beach
Whose pebbles rattle like a code, a sign
That language will be always out of reach
So asking why do these scenes fill my heart
Is answered by these flawed, cracked stabs at art.

AUTUMN

A sunset has been splashed across the sky
The colours seem too perfect to be real.
The clouds are sewn from blood and orange peel,
A paint-by-numbers yacht is sailing by
I'm slowly strolling on the sunlit sand
In one of those Septembers like a gift
From someone, somewhere. Hours seem to drift
In ways that I can never understand
But this is the best place to feel the move
From summer into autumn as the light
Does something subtle to the land and sea
And I stand by the shore as if to prove
That Autumn's colours filtered through my sight
Inhabit land and water, air and me.

WINTER

That rarest of moments: snow on a beach,
White moving driftwood, a seaweed that flies
Or seems to. Horizon just out of reach
Rendered unstable, its truth turned to lies
By these wind-flung clouds obscuring the view
Of anything solid. My thoughts are these:
Cold winter seasides can give us a clue
Of possible futures caught in the breeze
That might blow us away, far out to sea
Where land is a memory, mind-held, old
As the forests shrink to one broken tree
And the climate grips us in something cold.
Still, make a snowman then wait till the tide
Carries your art to the ocean's far side.

SPRING

Imagine these shells are new shoots growing
In the bright grin of March, early morning
With the wide sky like this walker, yawning.
The year whispers 'I know where I'm going'
And this sense of shift, of change, is growing
That spring is settling in with the dawning
Ignoring the half-light's shadowed warning.
The year is turning: the sea is glowing
On the blank page of newness. Seabirds bob
On the water like small trawlers sleeping
And dreaming of summer while now, and here,
The year's first clear morning does a fine job
Of riding through time on tide's horse, keeping
Track of the days as they stroll down the pier.

SUMMER

I make my way through crowds to find the sea;
The tide's internal clock tells it to turn.
A man stands like a withered flat-capped tree,
My grandad in a suit, his face set stern
Against the big idea that fills the beach:
The less you wear, the more you're having fun.
His ghost has come from somewhere out of reach
And stands there sweating in the mid-day sun.
That generation liked to button up,
Got off the train then walked down to the sands,
Poured strong tea from a flask into a cup
That seemed so tiny in their massive hands.
Then, gazing at the sky, they liked to sit
And contemplate one less day down the pit.

SNOW BEACH

Let's face it: you shouldn't have to walk down a beach in the snow. It feels wrong, unnatural. It feels like the opposite of a holiday. An anti-holiday. This snow isn't just the gentle tumbling stuff you see on Christmas cards either, it's snow as chucked by a knife thrower or fired from a snow cannon. It meets your wrapped-up-warm body and turns it into the inside of a fridge.

Look, who are these three hunched figures moving across the snowy sands like The Wise Men with a broken satnav? It's Ian McMillan and his wife and their ten-year-old grandson Thomas, who are on a pre-Easter break in Northumberland in their favourite cottage in Beadnell. All week the weather has been alternately sulky and angry; Ian and Thomas have played chess and all three of them have read and watched TV and, when the rain and sleet stopped briefly, they've ventured out on to the beach.

This time they took a football; the wind ignored the offside rule and ran all the way down the sands with it to give it an early bath. The snow was like a ticker-tape welcome. For some reason the three of them persisted in trying to play football perhaps because they were from Yorkshire and they'd bought the football and paid for the cottage and they were blooming well going to make use of them both.

The snow continued to fall. The sea, churned up by the wind, boiled and seethed in a genuinely scary way. Ian couldn't stop imagining himself in a small boat on that snowy ocean. Usually, at this point in a holiday by the sea, Ian will look at the sky that is the colour of a vest rejected by a charity shop and say 'Do you know, I think it's clearing up', much to the derision of those around him. The sky is so indifferent to persuasion today that Ian doesn't say it. The three snow people walk back to the favourite cottage and turn on the tiny television. They catch (like a chucked snowball) the weather forecast, which is grim. Grimness will fall spasmodically for the next couple of days and there will be a wind so grim it will try its very best to take your hair from your head and replace it on somebody else's. They have an early lunch of beans on toast, which already, somehow and in a faint kind of way, feels elegiac.

A rite of passage for people as young as our grandson was then and for people as middle-aged as Ian McMillan and his wife were then is the decision to go home early from the seaside holiday. This doesn't mean the emergency return, through illness or other misfortune, it means the (usually weather-based) moment of saying 'Look, this isn't going to work, is it? We may as well go home. It's not fun just being trapped in the cottage; we can sit in the house at home.' That snowy morning on the beach more or less convinced my wife and I that we should take that decision.

I don't know what the clincher was for my wife, but for me it was having to walk, almost bent double, into the gnashing teeth of the snow-decorated wind on the beach that did it. I felt like Captain Scott making his steady way to the North Pole or one of Father Christmas's reindeer reluctantly walking to the sleigh for the great annual journey. Thomas didn't seem to mind the wind and I gamely joined in his game of catching snowflakes until we got back to the wonderful otherworldly warmth of the cottage and the wind yodelling down the chimney.

The thing was that my wife and I had arrived at our 'let's go home early' decisions separately and neither of us wanted to tell the other one in case of disappointment. What if one of us wanted to stay? What then?

We sat in the cottage and did a jigsaw that, ironically, was of a sun-kissed rather than snow-snogged beach. As the last piece went in, by some miracle, it stopped snowing. The sun attempted to peep at us and the wind reclassified itself as a breeze. Maybe we wouldn't go home after all. Maybe it was a good thing that we took the decision separately, because once one of us had said the H word then a spell would have been broken and we would have had to go H.

'Let's have a drive into Seahouses and go to the Farne Gift Shop,' my wife said. The Farne Gift Shop is a treasure chest, an Aladdin's Cave, the internet with a roof on; it's everything you'd ever want to buy on a seaside holiday and much more besides. The sun was really out now, not pretending to be out. It was still achingly cold but we put layers on top of our layers and ventured out.

The car park in Seahouses, usually full, was almost empty. Out towards the East I could see that black ink had been spilt across the sky but I didn't mention it. We scuttled across to the Farne Gift Shop and took our time up and down its packed aisles. I bought a calendar that showed the places we'd been in the past few days but without snow and frost; my wife bought a fridge magnet for her mother. Thomas bought a huge toy car that appeared to spark from its exhaust. It seemed very bright in the shop, which meant it was very dark outside.

We exited into a blizzard that tried to steal my calendar but I hung on to it. We ran back to the car and drove back to the cottage. In the cottage Thomas played with his car and I put the kettle on. It was snowing again.

My wife and I, like people in a film, spoke at the same time. 'We should go home,' we said. Outside, the snow agreed.

LIKE A STATUE

My dad joined the Royal Navy in 1937 when he was eighteen, and left in 1958 because they offered him a desk job but you can't sail a desk. His life at sea was mysterious to me; perhaps that was because he left the navy when I was little but to my brother, who is seven years older than I am, and my mother, the Royal Navy loomed as huge as that white wave that envelops the crew at the end of Edgar Allan Poe's *The Narrative of Arthur Gordon Pym of Nantucket*, a book that I went back to and back to as a teenager, like I did to Herman Melville's *Moby-Dick* and Malcolm Lowry's *Ultramarine*, to try to work out what the sea was and what it meant to my gentle dad who loved to fish and dig his garden and wear a tie.

He liked fishing in trout streams and ponds and he enjoyed tying fishing flies and he liked picking blackberries but most of all he liked being near the sea, and because Barnsley is about as far away from the sea as you can get he liked going away to the seaside for his holidays. He also liked watching films and TV programmes about the sea but if there was something that wasn't factually accurate or that he thought portrayed the navy in a bad light he would shake his head and turn the TV off and start reading his *Trout & Salmon* magazine, the one he subscribed to and which would plop through the letterbox each month like a fish landing.

Once, the day before we went on a seaside holiday, the whole family sat and watched Alfred Hitchcock's *Lifeboat*, one of his odder films, which is entirely set on the eponymous vessel.

My dad had seen the film before and was really enjoying it, sometimes telling us what he thought was about to happen next and sometimes getting it right but not too often. My theory now, many decades on, is that he was just enjoying the motion of the boat on the waves and that he might have enjoyed an artist's video of waves in a darkened room in a gallery just as much, although he would never have visited a gallery to look at an artist's video.

As we watched there was a knock at the door. It wasn't late, but it was late for us, and me and my brother had our pyjamas on. My mother and dad looked at each other, unsure as to what to do. Hard to believe now but in those far-off days not many people had telephones and bad news was often preceded by a knock at the door that, when opened, would reveal a copper with his hat off.

This had happened when my dad's dad, known as Pappy, died. The knock came quite early in the morning and the copper was silhouetted in the sunlight that came through the glass in the front door. I recall the start of his words 'Regret to inform you that your father George McMillan…' and the rest of the sentence, in my memory, dissolved into weeping.

The door was knocked on again. The lifeboat continued to bob. My dad opened the door; I stood behind him and saw a man that the next day on the car journey to the coast my dad would describe as 'a gentleman of the road' standing there with a thin dog that looked like it had been dribbled on to the evening. The man said something that I couldn't catch and my dad nodded and went and got a bowl of water for the dog, which lapped greedily at it. My mam went into the kitchen and came back with some cake wrapped in foil that she gave to the man, who thanked her in a high, scratchy voice, then folded himself and the dog into the late summer evening. 'Who was that?' I asked, thinking that it might be somebody my parents knew from church. 'Just an old sailor down on his luck,' my dad said, closing the door. 'How did you know?' I asked, or my memory says that I asked. 'I could tell by the way he stood and by the way he spoke,' my dad said, 'and then when he walked away I really knew.'

It's true that, because he'd been at sea for so long, my dad still walked around the house as though he was on deck and for many years after he packed his uniform away in the wardrobe he still stood to attention after he'd finished his breakfast or his dinner.

On a beach, any beach, my dad could sometimes seem a bit distracted, a little abstracted from the noise and ice creams going on around him. He would stand like a statue gazing at the horizon that he had spent so much of his working life scanning. The big battle he was involved in during the Second World War was the one that sunk the German battleship *Bismarck*, and occasionally he could be persuaded to tell the story, of how they followed and destroyed it, although he told it reluctantly. Somehow the story still floated around untold, especially when we were on holiday and the tide was coming in. I think now that when we were at the seaside and the waves stretched as far back as the 1940s he would be looking at the past that knocked on the door like an old sailor down on his luck. And he would stand there until my mam told him it was time we were going.

SEEING THE SAND

For many years the cartoonist Tony Husband and I travelled up and down the country presenting our 'hilarious' (blurb word) show *A Cartoon History of Here* in village halls all over the B-road place; all we needed was a flip chart for Tony and a stage for me and we were up up and away. Sometimes we'd be what we laughingly called 'on tour', which meant that we were away from home for a couple of nights staying in people's spare bedrooms or small B&Bs or, occasionally (and these were my favourite), anonymous corporate hotels or (my second favourite) cottages by the sea. The late John Peel once said that listening to an album by the singer-songwriter Bridget St. John was like 'renting a cottage by the sea' and on the occasions when we woke up and put the kettle on in one of those beautiful kitchens, I thought that in some indefinable way our gig the night before had simply been a prelude to renting a cottage by the sea.

Once we stayed in a cottage in Perranporth, having done a gig at the local public hall; the next gig wasn't too far away and so it meant we had that rare thing, a day at leisure. Tony, of course, had cartoons to do; at that time he was doing a daily one for a national newspaper, which meant that at some point in the morning he would ring the paper to get an idea of which story they wanted him to do the cartoon for. We'd then find a café somewhere and Tony would sketch four ideas on a sheet of paper. We'd then have to find a fax machine; sometimes the café owner would have a fax that Tony would charm them into letting him use on the promise of a free cartoon. Sometimes we'd have to find a business centre, somewhere that would charge us. Tony would send the cartoons off and we'd then have time for a stroll before he'd get the call from the newspaper that said 'We like number three but can you make it funnier' and then we'd usually have to find another café and a scanner.

The stroll in Cornwall was on a windy beach that flung my hair around like somebody chucking a firework. Kites tried to escape to the USA. Gulls gave up the unequal struggle and just swam around in the deep end of the sky. Tony took photographs and waited for the call from the newspaper. We sat on a bench and had takeaway coffee, which the breeze almost took away. We went to a newsagent and Tony browsed the magazine section like he always did, buying a couple he hadn't come across before so that he could send them sample cartoons. I'm telling you all this like I'm reconstructing a crime scene because, as we walked back across the beach to the cottage, Tony began his familiar pocket-tapping dance that meant he'd lost his phone or his wallet or his keys or his glasses. It was inevitable, like the turning of the tide, that on one of our jaunts Tony would lose something. I glanced at him and he said 'I can't find my glasses'. Ah well, on a scale of one to ten the glasses are about a three. He wouldn't be able to see to draw his cartoons but at least he could ring people up about it and buy magazines in a shop and get into his car and drive it.

I began the ritual, the antiphonal chant. 'Do you remember when you last saw them?' 'No.' 'Did you have them on in that shop where you bought the *Yachting Monthly*?' 'I don't think so.' 'Did you have them on when we were sitting on that bench?' 'I can't remember.'

Visitors to the beach that windy day would have been treated to the sight of what looked like a pair of men in late middle age beachcombing, or two men in late middle age performing a piece of Live Art. We wandered up and down like wading birds, watching for the glint of the glasses. Every now and then we'd think we'd seen them but it would always turn out to be glass not glasses. We somehow hoped that if the sea had taken the glasses the sea might somehow give them back. Tony is a gregarious man who likes to talk to anyone and he would ask total strangers 'Have you seen my glasses?' and they would either ignore him completely or just say no. Then, amazingly, somebody said 'Yes', and fished a pair of glasses out of their pocket. 'I was just on my way to the police station with them.' Tony put them on; he looked like Elton John Live At The Hollywood Bowl. They weren't his but he kept them on just a couple of seconds too long before handing them back. I could see that he was tempted to say they were his.

So now, in an odd scenario like a black-and-white European film, there were two lost pairs of glasses and there could be two sets of people looking for them. We paced up and down as the tide came in and the time of our gig approached. The wind dropped and a kind of mocking mist strolled towards the fringes of the sea. I knew that we'd have to be going soon. Tony's phone rang and I half hoped it was his glasses ringing from a call box. It was the newspaper asking for his final version of the cartoon. We'd established earlier that the organiser of the gig that evening had a scanner so the plan was to get to the village hall a little early, draw the cartoon and then get the organiser to scan it at the same time as making us a cup of tea and a lovely sandwich.

We walked towards the car; people passing us would have seen that we were visibly agitated. Tony sneezed, put his hand in his pocket and pulled out a huge white hanky. And a pair of glasses, which fell on to the car park's tarmac with a guilty sound. Maybe, in some odd and indefinable way, the sea really had taken them and the sea really had given them back. Or sneezed them back.

YOU'LL WRITE A POEM
ABOUT THAT

I'm on the beach at Bamburgh in Northumberland, walking so slowly I'm convincing myself that time is just a human construct and it doesn't really exist at all; or maybe it exists temporarily like that sandcastle. Yes, of course time has no idea what a month is and couldn't care less how long a second takes to flicker by but I'm in such deep reverie on this wide sand canvas that I'm questioning the very nature of time itself. I'll give it a capital letter: of Time itself. That's what Northumberland does to me: it makes me aware of all kinds of possibilities and it convinces me that, in certain lights and at room temperature, I could have been a philosopher.

I'm also eating a bag of crisps so enthusiastically that many of them are transferring themselves to my polo shirt. I know, I'm a 65-year-old bloke and I shouldn't be eating a bag of crisps but I'm on my holidays and so I'll allow myself just the one bag, like I allow myself a tube of Pringles at Christmas. There's something reassuring to me that my mind is churning big Time-based thoughts around and my hands are conveying crisps into my eager mouth, missing the target more than once. I accidentally drop a crisp and a passing gull falls to the sand, picks up the crisp and steals it away in an excitement of wingflaps. A man in a hat too big for his head and probably for his lifestyle too points at the gull and says 'You'll write a poem about that!'

YOU'LL WRITE A POEM ABOUT THAT

Oh yes: the cry that fills the air whenever I'm around, whenever any poet is around, once people know you attempt to write deathless verse either as a hobby or as a living (and let's face it, as far as poetry is concerned the two aren't always so far apart). Those six words follow me everywhere; less so these days, to be honest, because I'm not on TV very much, but somebody always seems to spot me on a beach or at a beauty spot and, with a chuckle in their voice like a mid-morning DJ, they'll challenge me to put pen to paper. The Eiffel Tower, Niagara Falls, Wembley Way, Anglesey, Toronto, Clifton Park in Rotherham, Great Yarmouth: if I'd written a poem about all of them, I'd have an anthology full with some drafts to spare.

I grin at the bloke and his hat and say 'Yes, I might. Or a novel!' We both laugh and the gull wheels away. I could tell him all the things I'm about to tell you about the poem I think I'm going to write, but he's already halfway to Seahouses, walking so quickly he's almost catching up with the motion of the Earth so that where he is, it's standing still.

The thing is, I was going to write a poem about this moment on this beach. My notebook is folded and ready for action in my pocket and there's a pen rubber-banded to it that's brimming with unwritten lines. The poem I'm going to write will have something of the past in it, and something of this morning's reflected and refracted light. It will try and link the then and the now, try and get them walking alongside each other; perhaps that's where my earlier Time-thinking is going. Into a file marked IAN'S POEMS.

The poem won't rhyme, and the rhythm will be the rhythm of my speech and of my thoughts. It will be about the nature of change and how some things never seem to change at all. I find the coast a good place to begin poems but not to finish them, for some reason that maybe has to do with familiar settings rubbing up against unfamiliar settings to strike sparks that might eventually smoulder into a poem. I'll make notes and have a run-up and maybe a high jump or two into a couple of lines; the notes will be incoherent and inchoate and anybody stumbling across them, once they've wiped the gull poo and the chip grease away, will find something that looks like a half-formed shopping list or a prescription for corn plasters. Somewhere in these squiggles and biro-runes a poem is waiting in disguise.

At home, in my little writing room, I'll engineer the lines into some heavy lifting and gradually I'll be able to take the scaffolding away and the poem will stand on its own shaky metrical feet.

Now, though, the poem is just floating around in the Northumberland air. I stand by the water and remember the time my three kids and all their cousins ran up and down the beach endlessly one broad and beautiful summer, playing a game that they had devised and the rules for which they redevised every five minutes. The younger me stands next to my two brothers-in-law and if you were to do a reconstruction of the scene now, I would be the only surviving brother-in-law. The other two are not with us any more, on the beach or anywhere. They'll be in the poem, though; they'll have that paper and alphabet immortality. They'll be laughing as a Frisbee spins towards them.

The poem will partly be about loss and about the way each turning of the tide is a kind of loss. I still think every day about those two men on whom the tide went out. I write the word Frisbee in the notebook, making the poem's beginnings seem even more like a shopping list. As the waves lap my beach pumps, I make a solemn promise to myself and to the ghosts of Martyn and Terry that I won't make the Frisbee into a heavy-handed metaphor for something coming out of nowhere. Maybe the crisp-eating gull will feature, though; maybe I could pretend they were eating crisps. Maybe that slight incident, reshaped with added linguistic music, can pull its weight across a line or two.

As the man said, I'll write a poem about this.

PRE-CLEETHORPES DREAMING

It's April 2021 and the country is slowly unlocking; one Wednesday evening, on my way back from recording a radio programme in Salford, I call in at The Station Tap on Sheffield station and drink a gorgeous pint in the bracing open air. A man passes; he looks appreciatively at me pleasure-glugging. 'Just like being at Cleethorpes!' he says, indicating the ever-changing cityscape. I laugh. He notices my scarf. 'It'll be colder theer though,' he says. 'Allus cold in Cleethorpes!' I agree and feel a slight East Coast shiver. I can almost smell the fish and chips and the sea air. I pull my hat down further and gaze at the beer's gold glow.

My mother-in-law's caravan in Cleethorpes is unserviced, which means that she has to use shared facilities in the concrete toilet block across the field. This further means that she can't stay in her caravan until 17 May, a restriction she accepts stoically. She's spent her time getting things ready to take with her for The Great Unlocking. Others, with modern vans, can be walking on the tops and licking ice cream just as I'm sipping beer in Sheffield but my mother-in-law is still at home making transcendent egg custards and sublime rhubarb crumbles in between watching snooker and Westerns on her TV. Snooker and Western isn't a genre, by the way, although maybe it should be.

I got a taxi to the station the other day and usually the driver and I talk about football but this time he wanted to talk about his caravan in Cleethorpes; he'd been to visit it, to set it up ready for when he could stay. 'I had a walk on the front,' he says, 'and you could see all the way to the other side.' He repeats the phrase as I get out of the cab. 'You could see all the way to the other side.'

Seeing all the way to the other side is what this time of Cleethorpes-interregnum is all about for my mother-in-law and the taxi driver and anybody else who hasn't, in this uncertain and brittly joyous spring, been able to stay in their caravan yet.

We're still in the garden and I'm eating a slice of currant pasty, although I'm from Barnsley so I call them 'kerrens'. We're all trying to see all the way to the other side. I'm picturing this iconic walk along the tops that we always talk about even when we're doing it, the wind coming in from the sea so athletically that it's running rings around me and flapping my scarf like a flag on a yacht. I can hear myself trying to say something witty/poetic to my wife who is holding on to her hat but in the end neither of us can hear my aphorisms because the wind is shouting too much. My wife is picturing a moment when one of our daughters was a baby and we're pushing her along this path sometime in 1983 and the sun keeps playing hide-and-seek with the clouds.

She shouts the memory across to me and now I remember it too; we'd come for a few days at the caravan with our new baby because sleeplessness feels less punishing when there's sea air involved. We'd got a lovely buggy and I was always a proud dad when I pushed it down the street and people would lean into it and say lovely things. About the baby, obviously, not about me.

We'd bought a kind of movable parasol that fitted to the front of the buggy with a wing-nut attachment that seemed to me, as a deeply and proudly (well, it gets me out of changing fuses) impractical man, that even I could work. The idea was that if the sun shone too hard in the child's face, you just loosened the wing nut and adjusted the parasol and the shade was instant and sleep-inducing.

How young we all looked, because how young we all were! There was, as ever, a strong breeze that shoved the clouds around a side-plate-blue sky, so we made sure the parasol was secure as we headed out. We pushed South along the path towards the yacht club but somehow the sun, rather than the wind, kept changing direction and it seemed that every two minutes it hurled its blazing light into the baby's innocent face.

This meant that every two minutes we had to stop and adjust the wing nut and the parasol, but it seemed to us that every time we performed The Ceremony of Readjusting the sun was one step ahead of us and changed direction again, or it would skulk behind the clouds for a few seconds and then leap out to surprise us. That short walk on that sunny and windy morning has become part of our enduring family folklore. We often talk about it and exaggerate how many times we had to adjust that flipping parasol and how recalcitrant the wing nut became and how the passers-by gazed at us with a mixture of pity and, well, more pity. But the fact remains that I had to personally adjust that parasol at least ninety-five times. And that's no exaggeration.

Back in my mother-in-law's garden, I've finished the kerren pasty and we're laughing about the parasol and the wing nut from all those years ago. 'I'm sure we didn't alter it that many times', my wife says, but I'm not sure. Memory is a really interesting prism; you can see all the way to the other side.

APRIL 2021: ALMOST FORGETTING THE PIE

The day, the salt-sprayed and wide-beached day, has arrived. My wife and I are going to take her mother to check on her caravan in Cleethorpes and make preparations for the next Great Unlocking, which will happen in May and which will mean she can have, at the age of 92, yet another season in the sun. 2020's brief sojourn by the water was like a half-eaten sandwich that you have to leave on the plate because the café has suddenly been declared bankrupt and they're putting the chairs on the tables and turning the menus into paper aeroplanes and launching them around the kitchen.

She is part of what we've learned to call, in these tortured times, our bubble; she comes every Sunday for her Sunday dinner and praises my Yorkshire puddings but the talk inevitably turns to the weather in Cleethorpes and sometimes, between the Yorkshires and the main course, my wife will check her phone and read out the temperatures and wind speeds and predicted precipitation in Cleethorpes and even if it's freezing cold and blowing a gale my mother-in-law will say 'Aye, but it'll be lovely in front of that van' and I'll go and mash the potatoes. We are planning our trip and we're wondering about going for fish and chips and eating them in the caravan but my mother-in-law says 'It's OK, I'll make a pie' and my heart leaps at the thought of one of her wonderful meat and tatie pies. With mushy peas, of course. You've got to do it properly.

We pack the car with the curtains and blankets my mother-in-law brought home in October 2020, after her last Covid-curtailed season. We put coats and hats and scarves in while at the same time hoping we won't need them. It strikes me forcibly that this is almost the first time I've been to the coast since I started writing this book about the coast; I'm more excited than I can admit to anybody for fear of looking foolish but it's a bit like a cookbook writer must feel when they've been banned from the pantry for a while and they're finally allowed in.

We check the weather and it looks like it's going to be a freshly unwrapped day of the kind you might need wrapping up in. We set off and the coast is waiting to welcome us. We drive down a hill and turn a corner and we remark that the daffodils that brightened up the verge have gone over. There's a real sense that the world is turning. Just one more thing: spring is here and rattling towards summer. Come on: there are pies to be eaten and strolls to be strolled. There is silence in the car as we all project ourselves towards that sacred and liminal space where the tide meets the sand and they both meet your toes.

Suddenly my mother-in-law, from her nest on the back seat surrounded by bags and the little packet of biscuits she brings just in case, says, rhetorically, 'Have I brought the pie?' She fishes in the bag next to her that we all think the pie is in. It isn't there. We pull into a side street next to the River Dearne; oddly, it's only about half a mile from our house and I've lived in this village all my life but I've never been on this particular side street before. We look in the bag and in the boot but it's a fact. We're pieless. Crust almighty!

My wife turns round and we drive back; it strikes me, not for the first time as I piece this book together in these most extraordinary of years, that everything rings with metaphor even more than usual. We set off; we turn back. We lock down; we are unlocked. We advance a little; we retreat. People are allowed in the house then people are not allowed in the house. We think we have a pie but we do not have a pie.

We park outside mother-in-law's house and she goes in and then returns bearing the pie triumphantly as though it is part of the Crown Jewels like the sceptre and the orb. We put it on the back seat next to her so that now we have two precious passengers.

The route is simple and it is made up of lines like the back of my hand. It ends with the road down to the caravan. The sky is wide and welcoming and even the clouds seem to have been glued together with light. There's a bridge over the Trent that we call the Halfway Bridge even though it's not really halfway. My mother-in-law keeps an eye out for apple blossom and we speculate about the trees we'll see near the caravan; last year the lockdown must have been good for blossom because we harvested bag after bag of apples from the trees in the scrubland between the sand and the Fitties Bungalows where we occasionally saw a homeless man living in a tent. My mother-in-law would lean forward precariously, trying to hook one more fruit with her stick. Once, in the evening, when we were bringing her home for a few days, we saw some deer like nervous and uncertain shadows; they seem to have been etched on the air and now whenever we go to the caravan or return from the caravan we look for the deer and we never see them. But, if everything is metaphor, then maybe seeing them once is enough and the rest is just resonance and humming.

Suddenly we can smell the fish fingers and we know we're nearly there. And we pass Grimsby Town's ground, Blundell Park, and we know we're even more nearly there. And we pass the leisure centre and the light railway and we turn down into the camp. We're there. We're here. We've got a pie.

DRUGGED BY THE PIE

Having arrived in Cleethorpes, my wife and I go for a stroll along the tops and the sky, as it should be, is almost too wide for the sky. Boats that look like toys amble up and down the Humber and a scattering of oystercatchers face the slight breeze and let it minimally redesign their feathers. A man walks past and says to a woman, 'I don't know why you're bothering, they're not even close friends. They're just friends.' A masked woman trundles by on an electric scooter. If the speed of light was powered by a fully charged battery, she would be faster than the speed of light. She buzzes like a metal wasp and nods at me to acknowledge that she knows I know that she's buzzing like a metal wasp. What she doesn't know is that she's about to buzz into a page of a book.

My mother-in-law is in the caravan getting a few ornaments out ready for the start of the season; like a kind of grammar or syntax, the act of getting out the artefacts reminds her where they go on the shelves, just as the act of getting the words out to put into a sentence reminds you where go they. Reminds you where they go. We walk to where the ice-cream man often is but isn't there yet because of the pandemic and in my head I am rehearsing the taste of the first 99 of the season. The first of ninety-nine 99s one year, I hope. You can tell that I'm a bit giddy because spring is here or hereabouts.

I tell my wife, only half joking, that I can smell the pie. We begin to stroll back to the caravan. Now I really can smell the pie, or the anticipation of the pie. I'm an emotional man and as I walk I almost begin to well up; the winter has been so long and its grip has been so tight. The deaths have been relentless and the social distancing has become a habit of mind and there were times when it got so dark, metaphorically and really, at 4pm that I thought I'd never get to walk by this mud and that sea as flat as the last scene of a film you guessed the ending of. I thought that this book would be all memories, that the coast itself would just become an aspiration and an inspiration rather than somewhere I could get between my toes.

Back at the caravan many of the ornaments are in place but, more importantly, the pie is just about to come out of the oven and the peas are on the hob. 'There's a burnt bit of crust for you' my mother-in-law says, and my happiness is almost complete. Maybe this is worth the dark winter. It's an odd thing, and maybe a Yorkshire thing, this enjoying of the burnt bits. When I get to our local bakery and I ask if they've got any loaves with the crusts a bit burnt, I'm always too late. Other charry-aficionados have got there first.

The pie emerges. There's a burnt segment like a black collar on a pale shirt. I am a happy man. The mushy peas have arrived from heaven. The gravy has the ability to make you into a better human being, or so it seems. We sit down to eat. Like a child at a party I save the best, the burnt bit, till last. It's exquisite.

Then, even though I know I shouldn't, I make the mistake of accepting a second portion of pie, this time without the singed bit because I've eaten all of that. Even as I munch I feel a yawn brewing at the back of my jaw. I'm aware that my eyes are starting to fail some kind of test. I get up very early every day; I usually wake up at about 4.30am feeling marvellous. I spring out of bed at 5am (having composed several lines of poetry in my head) and go for my early stroll. I get back in the house at 6.06 and do some exercises involving grunting and small weights. I still feel tiptop.

This tiptoppery lasts until about 1pm and then, particularly if I've eaten loads like I just have, I start to slump. Gravity attacks my eyelids.

I can feel myself starting to go; I am a house of cards that is about to tumble. I am an argument that is about to be demolished by better debaters than me. That second plateful. I shouldn't have had it! After the second helping, I'd made the tactical and probably strategic error of moving to the settee. I force myself vertical and sit on a hard seat at the dining table but I begin to list to one side; I am about to sink. I see my wife and mother-in-law exchange glances that seem to underline that I am more to be pitied than blamed. My wife often says that I should spend another hour in bed but then I'd miss out on lots of tiptoppery.

I decide to go back to the settee and rest my eyes for a moment. Just for a moment. I fall into a sleep so deep it is as though I have been mummified. I dream a vivid and knife-sharp dream about a visit to the caravan when my children were little and my younger daughter had a cough that worsened and worsened as the evening wore on until we had to take her to hospital in Grimsby. We stayed overnight and I slept beside her in a bed made of rocks. Before we went to sleep I told her stories about the places we'd go the next day; to the sands, to Mr Ben's for ice cream, to the amusement place we called HillyBilly Moonshine, to the little train with its open carriages that let the weather sit beside you. And of course she got better the next day. In the spring of 2020 she got coronavirus and I remembered the croup and the overnight stay and I was scared. Luckily, after a few days she recovered. That hospital bed, though. That steel mattress.

Leave me here for a moment, will you, dreaming? It'll soon be time to stroll by the water again.

THE RUNNING MAN

A combination of the sea air on the Northumberland coast and an increasing knowledge of my advancing age have convinced me that, rather than just strolling down the wide beach near our holiday cottage in the early morning, I should run. I should become, for those brief minutes in the sun, a running man. Bear in mind that although I walk a lot and I feel quite fit and healthy, I have hardly run anywhere except when I have had to run for trains or buses and then my action would be more of a totter or a galumph or, if we're being picky and specific, a totter-galumph. And of course, running on the beach I wouldn't be able to do that 'I'm not running' run that we've all done when we've TG'd for a double-decker that has seen us coming and pulled away from the stand.

I put my sand shoes out the night before in an attempt to convince myself that I would actually do the run. My wife sensibly pointed out that I wasn't a runner and that I could, in her very image-laden phrase, 'do myself some damage'. That night, which never really seemed to get dark because it was June, I had a strange dream; perhaps it could be interpreted as an anxiety dream about my jogging aubade but it didn't feel like it when I woke up and the dream was still as real as a spider on the ceiling. In the dream I was sitting in a chair in the very cottage we were renting and I was translating a book of poetry from a language that was so endangered it was only spoken by the person who'd written the poems and who was, according to the vivid and widescreen logic of the poem, on her deathbed. I remember that in the dream I had read one line aloud: 'The small streets are too tight for my boots.' Anxiety? Well maybe.

And then, as they say in the best fairy tales, I woke up. I padded through to where I'd left my sand shoes. Yes, they're not the kind of shoes anybody who'd ever been on a run would go running in but I point you to the middle-aged man making his legs go as fast as they can as a bus pulls slowly away from a suburban stop. The sun already feels escaped-balloon high. It's warm and I put my sand shoes on. I feel a sense of excitement when maybe I should have been feeling a sense of dread. You'll see that, like the translator I was in my interrupted dream, I'm flip-flopping around past and present tense.

I walk towards the beach because of course you have to walk before you can run. I envision a future me with sculpted stomach muscles although I'm not sure if you can translate running into stomach muscles, but I'll give it a good go.

I'm so early that there are no dog walkers about, which is good because I'm not, in my mother's phrase, dog-fond. I didn't want to be chased by one and then be told by its owner that 'It's as soft as a brush'. Well, that's as maybe, but even soft brushes can be dangerous when you're bending over gasping for breath.

I find myself in what I'm guessing experienced runners might call a 'pre-run state'. I stand still. I bend and stretch like I've seen runners do. I look like I have failed a contemporary dance exam.

Suddenly (because I sense that this is the only way to do it) I hurl myself into a run. One moment I am motionless and the next moment I am motionful. It is comparable to one of those times in the development of moving film when great strides are made very quickly. My strides aren't great but they are functional. I am running. For the first time since I was a young man and got heckled from passing cars by youths, I am running for exercise.

The beach is vast but my pounding feet are covering it with speed. Maybe I am going too quickly; perhaps I am going too slowly. I have no idea what the correct speed is. Some dog walkers have appeared at the far end of the beach. I hope their dogs don't decide to chase me because I have an instinctive grasp of the fact that no matter how fast I ran, even the oldest dog in the North of England would be able to catch me easily.

What's that noise? A bellows is revving up to get an old church organ going before the congregation troop in; an old elephant is blowing air through its leathery trunk. Someone is scraping wallpaper from a wall using the bluntest of instruments; a mountain is clearing its throat. No, none of the above: my lungs are straining loudly to keep up with my feet.

I feel exhilarated and anxious at the same time; surely I shouldn't be breathing this loudly? Surely I should have made some progress down the beach? Surely the sea should be a little bit closer rather than a little bit further away? But still, I'm running. I'm running across the sand and this must be doing me just as much good as my endless early morning and late evening strolls.

Then in the blink of an eye and the click of an ankle (or vice versa) I am posted through a letterbox marked pain. I've slipped on some seaweed and my ankle has jarred a little and I grind through some gears and come to a halt. I hop a few times, and then tentatively put my weight on my ankle. It hurts, but not too much. I limp back to the holiday cottage, my pride smarting.

O beach the size of a county, do not laugh at me behind my back! O wide, wide sky, forgive my middle-aged hubris! O running dogs, ignore the person who limps by the sea; you're right, it's best to believe he was never there! As it almost said in my dream, the wide beach is too slack for my sand shoes. Now where's that settee?

DON'T TOUCH THE SIDES
OF THAT TENT

Rain. Rain. Rain. Let me say it again, savouring the syllable, letting it wash (ha!) over my tongue. The way it starts and ends with soft consonants. The way the two vowels lean into each other like lovers might on a drizzly stroll. A small word for a huge thing that soaks into our thinking and dampens our language. A word you can take your time with, try and find the etymology of, then start singing 'Singin' in the rain' and 'Raindrops keep falling on my head' on an endless loop that turns like a mill wheel. The 'n' at the end of the word seems to land on your head like a raindrop might, soaking into your brain like rain does. It seems like a small word for such a big thing, such a life-enhancing thing in many ways, unless you've just got a week off and you're halfway through that week and it hasn't stopped stair-rodding once. In Yorkshire we say that it's 'siling it down' and I like that word 'siling' because it seems to me that somewhere within it there is a hidden splash just waiting to soak you.

There's plenty of time to play all these philosopho-linguistic games because, of course, it's raining. You're at the seaside, any British seaside, and it's raining. Remind me, just remind me, who thought it would be a good idea to go camping in a site by the side of a railway line where the first rain-splashed train rattled by at 6am? Ah yes, that would be me. Just don't touch the side of the tent. Don't touch the side of the tent! Too late. The tent is weeping. The train is passing. The train is hooting. The tent is soaking.

We've all suffered or enjoyed those rainy days by the coast. We've huddled in shelters as the rain King-Leared all over the show and rolled our eyes and said, with irony so heavy you could hold a gate shut with it, 'Why go abroad?' An elderly lady beside you in a rainmate will laugh a subterranean laugh that dies on contact with the outside world. That tent by the railway line was many years ago but I still recall it with a shudder.

Now the scene shifts to me as a grown man with children, and the rain tropes just keep on coming. As we've driven into driving rain and the kids have been restless in the back seat, we've all pointed to a patch of sky that seems slightly less grey than the rest and said those five words that seem already doomed as soon as you say them: 'I think it's brightening up...' The way those words hang in the air as though they are real.

Sometimes, of course, it doesn't feel like it's going to rain. The day begins as blue as a promise. You pack a picnic. You pack, despite the fact you said you never would after that greenhouse skirmish, a Frisbee. You pack a rug to sit on and there's a flask in there somewhere. For once you don't take anything to keep off the rain. The children are small so this is the distant time before you could check the weather on your smartphone and it would tell you exactly when it was going to rain and, if you had the upgraded app, how many raindrops would roll down the back of your neck. The weather today would have been checked on a tiny black-and-white TV in a holiday cottage or, amazingly, in a weekly local newspaper. That's right: a weekly local newspaper printed the preceding Friday. Both those sources said it wasn't to rain, and we believed them. Mind you, the screen on the TV was only as big as an ace of diamonds.

My parents always read the *Daily Mirror* but whenever we went on holiday my dad always insisted on buying the *Daily Telegraph* because, in his words, 'the weather is better'.

So you walk on to the dry beach and gambolling begins. Sandcastles spring up, designed by child architects. An ice cream is eaten although, inevitably, one is dropped into the sand, flake-down. We are all so intent on our fun that nobody notices the cloud approaching across the sea. The cloud that is as dark as a slug or a funeral hat. The cloud that takes its time because it knows that spoiling a family's day is a marathon not a sprint.

Gradually the air changes. There is a kind of fridge-door chill. A breeze touches your face a little too intimately. A single raindrop lands on your glasses like a ladybird once did. You look up and the sky is wearing its away kit. The rain begins, like a multiplication table: One drop is drop, two drops are splash, three drops are damp, all the way up to ten thousand drops which, as we all know, are soak.

The retreat begins. The gathering up of rugs and bags and spades and buckets and children. The rain falls on all of us equally and we begin to run. We're not the only ones caught out, of course: the beach is a diorama of running and the odd bit of screaming. It's like a deleted scene from *Jaws*. I shout, at the top of my voice, 'Why go abroad?' and this time there is no laughter from anywhere. A sudden thump of thunder rattles the sky's frame. A zig of lightning joins a zag. Now we are all properly soaked; my shirt sticks to me and does not want to let me go. My wife's trousers are a river in torrent. We all look like that stage of evolution when fish walked out of the sea to test out dry land.

The cloud races by and by the time we are back at the car the rain has slowed to a chunter. We open the doors and slide in, soaking the seats with our soakingness. 'I think it's brightening up,' I say. There is no reply.

WHAT THE WEATHER SAID

May 2021 on the surface of the spinning globe; well, on one particular scrap of the surface of the spinning globe, the scrap that connects South Yorkshire to Cleethorpes, connects hopes and dreams to reality; connects, for the mother-in-law, a lockdown winter with a summer that with a bit of luck will include trips from the caravan site to Grimsby on the bus on a sunny day with the sea reflecting the sky as though it's auditioning for a calendar.

My mother-in-law has been ready to go to her caravan for weeks but the weather hasn't been ready for her to go. It reminds me of those times when, as a boy, I would be knotted with anticipation as I waited for news of another rocket launch from NASA because I was a boy who loved rocket launches because they felt like a noisier and shinier version of real life than the one I was living in the South Yorkshire coalfield. Every so often the weather or a mechanical glitch would cause the postponement of the launch and it felt at that moment that the carefully constructed tent of my world had had the pegs pulled out. It was the same for my mother-in-law, without the countdown and the thrust.

We planned to take her to the caravan on a Monday but the rain was incessant and apocalyptic. We planned to go on a Tuesday but the drizzle was a stolid, chuntering presence. Wednesday wept and Thursday had a sky that watered like an eye. My wife and I would go to her house after our afternoon stroll and my mother-in-law would, after she'd put the kettle on, say 'I listened on the wireless to what the weather said and it didn't sound good.' It was as though the weather was speaking, bringing bad news of unfurling umbrellas and muddy paths to caravans. I imagined the weather speaking in a thundery voice that occasionally trickled with moisture.

Historians of the weather in the pandemic will note that, in the UK, the spring and summer of 2020 was glorious and mild, maybe (as many people said at the time) because we couldn't go anywhere and we had to watch the weather through the window or (if we were lucky) our gardens; they will also note that April 2021, when we all began to shudder into a tentative reopening that we hoped wouldn't be postponed like a NASA mission, the weather was bad. The start of May was an improvement on that but that's like saying that opening a tin of mushy peas and eating them cold with a fork is an improvement on not opening a tin of mushy peas and eating them straight from the tin with a fork.

The rain signs the windows like an artist. But then the weather says there will be a break in the clouds and the sun might stare through. So it's decided, on the Yorkshire version of a whim, to go the next day. My mother-in-law celebrates, as you'll have realised by now, by making a pie. The only fly in the ointment is the fact that I won't be able to go because I'm working that day; still, my wife will bring back me a slice of pie but it won't taste the same when I can't sprinkle it with sea air.

But then the weather speaks again, in a loud and stentorian voice, and the weather says it's going to rain again, all day, and the trip is postponed until the next day, which is a day I can go. Perhaps it's that rain dance I did in the garden. I hope so.

The following day does as it's told by the weather and the sun strides out to bat. My wife and I call at her mother's to pick up the 'last few bits', as they call them, to take to the caravan. And of course we, following our experience earlier in the year on a shorter visit, need to remind her to pick up the pie. Those three words 'last few bits' are a euphemism. A huge euphemism; indeed, she is taking so much stuff that I'm surprised her house doesn't float away just after she's locked the door. 'There's just a few bits upstairs. Watch your back,' she says and I bring the bags down. And the other bags down. And that last bag, which is probably the biggest bag, down.

The car boot is full and the area around my mother-in-law on the back seat is packed. The bags are in. The hoover is in. The tins are in. The TV, with a small screen about as big as an iPad's, is in. In her unserviced caravan she has to rely on solar power and a trek to a tap for water. And she takes all these provisions because she's 92 and although she's hoping to get to the shops on the bus, she can't carry loads and loads of shopping any more. It'll just be a few bits. Now, where have I heard that phrase before?

I like watching subtitled films where nothing much happens. Someone will gaze out of a window. A couple will sit at a pavement café sipping coffee. One of them will light a cigarette. Somebody may or may not walk by. It strikes me that this is what our trips to Cleethorpes are like; they aren't adventurous and they don't break new ground, indeed they enjoy going carefully over old ground. In this sense, they are like the coast I'm writing about: change happens slowly round there. Water becomes dunes and vice versa. That painted bike on the cycle lane fades slowly, becoming more like a ghost bike each year. The forts in the estuary grow rustier and rustier. The little train runs on its little rails. And my mother-in-law packs her bags and goes for the summer. And the weather says kind and gentle things. We hope.

EATING CHIPS BY THE SEA,
A RHAPSODY

The gulls tell you; the gulls know. The gulls have ancient chip-knowledge. Their sharp beaks; their silhouettes, altered by the jut of a chip. This street, reflecting the sealight and the skylight, is filled with chip shops. Fish and chip shops from fishing ships. The gulls know because here they wheel, here they come wheeling. There they disperse, there they show no interest at all; they are like bored teenagers at a relative's artexed bungalow that has no Wi-Fi. I have heard (I'm whispering now, and your ear is close, so close that you can hear the sea) that some people go into these coastal chip shops and order sausage. Yes, and they order pie. The gulls know.

Perhaps you ignore the gulls and want to make your own decisions. How, then, do you choose a chip shop? Is it the one you've been in so many times before that there are spaces on the lino where your sandy feet go and if you asked hard enough they could remember you as a little boy? Is it the one you used to go in that slithered downhill until you didn't want to go in any more but now it's changed hands so it might be better? Is it that one with the big queue or that one with the small queue? That one with the flock of gulls or that one with the feathered loner? If you're here by the sea for the day, the choice is more crucial; if you're on holiday for a week then you pick and choose. If you live here then you know; follow the ones who live here. They're the ones without sunburn sunsets on their necks, the ones in suits who've come straight from work. Follow them. The gulls will. There are vinegar stains on that man's jacket. Follow him.

Now the chip shop is chosen. The momentous moment. The queue is long but moving. You can hear, even from this distance, the sizzle of the fryer. Your eyes can detect that it's a Stott's Of Oldham, one of the best, a workhorse of frying that has pleasing modernist lines. An extra loud sizzle as a bucket of pale chips is poured in.

A sudden childhood memory: in an alley behind a chip shop at the seaside because we've got lost. The alley is lit by an evening's glow. The alley is narrow and my mam and dad and my brother and me are almost squeezed by its walls. At the end of the alley, a figure dressed all in white. Even the wellies are white, like ghost wellies. The figure is sitting on a wooden stool that seems older than time. The figure is wielding a knife that glints in the aforementioned evening's glow. We hesitate for a moment but then we see the potato in the non-knife hand. We see the pile of unpeeled potatoes. We see the sack with more unpeeled potatoes in. We squeeze past the potato peeler. My dad says 'Hello' to the potato peeler because he says hello to everybody whether he knows them or not, whether they're holding a knife and a potato or not. In my memory the potato peeler has at least one finger missing but I must be making that up because at the time of the alley encounter I was going through my Pan Book of Horror Stories phase.

You are in the queue behind a man whose vest fitted him at the start of his holiday a few days ago. Now he bulges a long way out of it and it tries to hold his breath. His neck is redder than spilled ketchup. His bald head is a shiny balloon of sweat. Maybe when he gets to the counter he will say 'The usual' and that will explain a lot. Someone comes in and shouts, in a voice that sounds like it hurts, 'Can you put me a tail in?', which is a phrase I haven't heard for years. As you inch closer to the Stott's the shop gets hotter and louder, almost drowning out the gulls outside. I have a brief fantasy about a gull getting dressed up as a holidaymaker to get closer to the centre, closer to the motherchip.

I'm at the front of the queue. I'm disappointed that the vestee didn't, in fact, say 'The usual'. In the Barnsley way, I just say 'Twice open, please' and the person behind the counter knows what I mean. I put some vinegar on but no salt because I'm a man in his mid-sixties and then I go outside into the seaside sun. Gulls form a guard of honour and I bravely stride past them. Already, because the tide is coming in, the fish and chips smell better than any fish or chips have ever smelled in the history of the world. Somehow it's as though the fish has carried the essence of the sea with it; somehow the batter is like a precious material. Somehow the chips are both crinkly and soft at the same time. Somehow, even though I asked for a small portion, there are more chips here than I could ever eat.

I make a silly error because I am drunk on vinegar and sunshine. I throw a chip in the air and a gull catches it. Then (I'm guessing here, but I'm not too far off) three million gulls arrive in the hope of a slam-dunked chip. The noise is tremendous and I walk towards the sea looking like a tractor in a field followed by shrieking gulls. There is a breeze in the air. There is the smell of sunblock and the whiff of yesterday's ale from the open door of a pub. I eat my chips and this is a kind of communion. I'm participating in a holy act. A pigeon poos on my shoulder but I don't care. I think I'll go back tomorrow and get more. With mushy peas this time; try and pinch *them*, gull-bullies!

ISLANDS OF MIDGES AND WASPS

I often dream of islands because they seem to be festivals of coastlines; they are all coastline with a bit of middle, like the distorted opposite of a Polo mint. As a child I would make lists of islands in red Silvine exercise books that my mother brought from Jack Brooks the Newsagent; I thought he was a spy and that he got the books directly from the government because he was an agent of news. Those island names, like one-word poems: Raasay, Hoy, Yell, Unst, Benbecula, Wight, Man, written down the page in my messy hand like characters in a folk tale.

Two islands soak into my memory, although I admit they didn't make my list even though both have resonant names: Skye and Caldy, one off the coast of North-West Scotland and one within touching distance of Tenby in South Wales. Although these two islands are very different, my memories of them are remarkably similar. They both involve vivid images of my parents running and waving, surrounded by insects that seem to scribble all over the air around them. To many people, Caldy and Skye are islands; to my family they were triggers for anecdotes about midges and wasps. Towards the end of his life, rendered immobile by a cruel stroke, my dad was sitting in his chair watching TV when a programme about Caldy Island came on and my dad began to wave his arms around his head in a way that alarmed Trevor the ponytailed carer until I explained about the wasps and we all laughed in that way that people thrown

together in somebody's twilight weeks often do. I could tell, by
looking at his distorted face, that my dad was back there on that
island in the early 1960s with the ice cream melting all over his
waving hand.

We were staying in Tenby with my Auntie Mary and Uncle Jack,
our constant holiday companions at that time. One day we decided,
on the recommendation of a man we'd met in a café, to take a trip
to Caldy Island to have a look at the monastery and sample some
of the ice cream that the monks made. I remember vividly that the
man said 'That ice cream, it's bloody good' and my dad tutted at
the word and my mam shook her head. Still, that didn't put us off
and we chugged over the water on a packed boat that bounced a
little bit, which reminded my dad of his years at sea. In my head I
kept saying 'Bloody good, bloody good' but of course I daren't say
it aloud. Especially not on a boat. No bloody chance.

We landed and wandered around the island; it didn't take
long and in my memory it was about as big as a giant vole. We
kept seeing people licking ice creams and we knew, because my
parents loved the idea of deferred gratification because they'd
lived through the war, that our reward for the wander, in a
kind of intense heat that brought a noisy storm later, would
be an ice cream as big as a Christmas tree. Maybe we noticed
people semaphoring a bit, their arms waving as though they
were guiding passenger planes into Tenby International airport,
but maybe that's just a bit of false memory that's melted and
dripped down my mind's sleeve.

The incidents of the late afternoon aren't false memory, though.
Not at all. Our wander ended and we queued for the ice cream. It
was still and monks sweated by in thick robes. The sun shone, as
Dylan Thomas might have said, in Welsh.

We got our ice creams, huge cumulonimbus numbers, and went
to sit down around a picnic table on benches that had suddenly
become free when a family moved away quickly, shrieking.

When a family moved away, shrieking. Maybe we should have taken more notice of that noisy egress but we were too busy thinking ice-cream thoughts. We sat down. Something buzzed. A wasp flew by. Then another, and another. They looked huge. Were they coming out of the sea? Were they some kind of mutant merwasp? One dived at my mother as though they were both cartoon characters and the messy exit that has been a mainstay of our family stories began.

Imagine this wasp-tale humming along in the background with a kind of split-screen effect while somewhere another similar story is happening many years later, when I am a teenager with a girlfriend who is now my wife of many years. We are with my mam and dad and we are on the Isle of Skye. It is the early evening and a blood-orange sun is sinking into the sea. We are sitting in the car drinking coffee from a flask and eating biscuits and my dad has put his waders on and his hat with fishing flies around the brim and he has wandered down to the edge of a loch that spills into the sea to do a bit of fishing.

In the car, as parents do, my mam is trying to embarrass me by telling tales of my childhood and she has begun the long and winding anecdote about the day the wasps came for the ice cream when suddenly my dad appears from down by the loch; it is as though runes are being visibly whispered around his head and he is waving frantically and actually hitting himself on the head like a self-trepanning novelty act. Despite his Scottish blood, the midges are going for him in a big way and he has admitted defeat. He runs, as best he can in waders, towards the car and makes the mistake (as my mother reminded him for decades after) of getting into the car and bringing the midges with him. Oh how they enjoyed our soft Yorkshire flesh! Oh how we wished that they were vegans!

Here the screen freezes; the midges in the car, the wasps with the monks in the background, the people who are simultaneously older and younger. From some angles the midges are landing in the ice cream, from some angles the wasps are invading the waders.

I remember now: memory is an eroding coastline.

BEING A CURATOR

Here is the exhibition; it will be held in The Kitchen Gallery for a very short time, so make sure you get to see it. There's a private view round about now so that's why I've got the kettle on. The exhibition is a mixture of realistic found work and fantasy pieces. There's some conceptual art and some photography and some language-based fragments. The kettle's about to boil. Anybody want a bun? All the pieces are for sale, by the way. Got to pay for the holiday somehow. We got back yesterday and it's still swirling round my head; its tide will soon be receding but for now it's in.

There isn't a catalogue for the exhibition but I can tell you that this first piece is a kind of dynamic interactive event. I'll just empty these sandals on to this doormat. Then I'll empty these other sandals and the wellies that some people wore on that damp day. I know; I should have emptied them outside, but I'm an artist.

See how what could be almost an entire beach piles up. I bet you could make sandcastles or at least the decimated ruins of sandcastles from this stolen sand from stolen moments. Sand aficionados would know that this sand came from several different beaches in a number of different weathers, and that the gathering of all these sands in the wellies and the sandals (hence the name, of course. Or maybe not.) is a kind of artistic intervention. Imagine the Sisyphian task of separating the grains and taking them back to where they belong, to address a kind of sand-lack. There are people at the private view (well, my family) chatting the kind of arty small talk you get at these events. Someone asks how many grains of sand there are on the mat. Someone of a more practical frame of mind reminds the spiller that they'll have to do some sweeping later, which is a bit like reminding Dalí that he'll have to tidy up those melting watches.

The second piece in the exhibition is the postcard that you forgot to send and which turned up in your cagoule pocket when you got home. It's a time capsule from the first two days of the holiday, which were drizzly and grey. The message is gnomic and haiku-like: 'Weather not great. Been to the slots. Sunny tomorrow.' I like the shift from despair to optimism in those few words, a lesson in style and concision for poets everywhere. The postcard is stood up on the windowsill where it catches the light. Is it worth posting it now, is the philosophical question that is on everybody's lips. Well, mine. The person it is intended for lives quite a long way away so they won't know if we're home or not. Perhaps it would be worth saving for another year. Perhaps it would be worth sending at some incongruous time like Christmas. That would make it a kind of Mail Art, that branch of art that trundles across the world powered by stamps and DIY optimism.

I sit at the table to sup tea and run a few holiday videos in my head. The table wobbles and a tear of tea rolls down the mug's face, or the mug's mug. Now I know what I can do with the postcard: I take it from the shelf, fold it into four and put it under the table leg, steadying it and stopping the mug weeping. Art can be practical, of course: it's not all gossamer wings and the shock of the new.

Next in the exhibition I'm curating comes a lovely piece that is a lesson in instant nostalgia: a fishing net and a red plastic bucket full of shells. Even last week, as you took the bucket and the net back to the car after the day on the beach, they were totems of some idealised past, a beach day that you will talk about for months, if not years, to come. The way the kids collected shells for hours. The way the shells rattled into the bucket. The way the kids stood together looking out to sea for just long enough to photograph. The way we kept holding shells to our ears to hear the sea. The way we decided to hold shells to our eyes to see the sea. The way we decided to hold shells to our noses to smell the sea. The way one of the kids danced when she found a ten-pence piece. The way I told her that if she held it to her ear she could hear rich people singing, and we both tried it before she put it in her purse.

The net is fragile and there is an aromatic/stinky line of seaweed wrapped around it that seems lost in the landlocked air. The net of the net is blue and it is so torn that it is hanging like an old circus poster that remains long after the show has moved on. It stayed in the car boot for a few days and I took it out tentatively because if the net tore completely away then what would I be left with? Can you call a net a net if it is just a stick and the net bit of the net is nowhere near the stick? Is it a net kit? Maybe as part of the exhibition the visitors to the gallery could be encouraged to make their own net? Let's face it, it's not that hard. On its own the stick has a kind of poignancy, as does the netty bit; together they are completely net, apart they are, well, nothing really. Two blank canvases waiting patiently for meaning.

The private view is almost over. Someone has said that the old net needs to go in the bin and we'll get a new one next time we go to the seaside. The shells are staying in the bucket. The card will continue to steady the table. Art, eh? It is what I say it is.

INTO THE WIND

My wife and I decide to have a walk along the wide and endless beach at Alnmouth in Northumberland. In some senses the coast is a complex thing, a layering of histories and stories and memory that is hard to unravel without the aid of spreadsheets and highlighter pens. In another sense the coast is a simple thing: it is a walk by the sea.

I like the car park at Alnmouth; you drive down a long path and someone gets out of a hut where they are doing a word search (a handy metaphor for the lot of the writer. I'll save it.) and you pay three pounds and you can stay all day. It's one of those mornings when it's hard to know what to wear and a glance at the people on the beach doesn't help. There are people in shorts and vests and people in cagoules; there's a topless bloke and a woman in a woolly hat. A cardigan hangs low; a pair of socks are pulled high. A headscarf decorates a head and an anorak defines a body. I've got my shorts on but my trousers are in the car boot; I elect to keep my shorts on. Spoiler: I regret this later. My wife is wearing a substantial coat. Neither of us have brought woolly hats because, dammit, it's June and the woolly hats have been sent to the old shoebox in the wardrobe where they'll live until the autumn. And no, we don't keep our winter shoes in a hatbox.

Behind us, golfers are dividing time into holes. A gentle breeze murmurs to the branches. A golf trolley passes. I notice, not for the first time, that the days when everybody had a dog have long gone; everybody has four dogs. I don't mind the idea of dogs in the abstract; dogs in poems or dogs in comedy films I can put up with. I guess it's just that I don't agree that dogs understand every word you say; I've tried them with *The Waste Land* and I can report they don't get it. The beach is dogfull and, like the people, some have coats on and some do not.

We walk down to the beach. The sky is the colour of your old school protractor, the one that you inexplicably kept until your thirties. There's a breeze that threatens to mock my shorts but, even though we're close enough to the car for me to go and put my trousers on, I choose to ignore it. Somehow as we stroll we can tell that the tide is turning. And another thing: it's getting chilly. The wind is getting up, stretching, deciding to go for a run.

The wind is colder than we thought it would be, or rather it's colder than I thought it would be because my wife has got her big coat on. We walk away from the wind and we are propelled along like land yachts. It's pleasant and I tell a passing quartet of dogs this but they don't understand. The sea is wearing a bundle of yachts like fascinators. A man chases a kite down the sands like men have chased kites down the sands for many many years. He may as well chase a gull.

Occasionally the sand gives my bare calves a caning, which is a reminder that fairly soon we will have to turn round and face the music; the wind music. I say 'We'll turn around when we get to that family huddling behind that windbreak' and my wife nods. We both think that the windbreak huddlers are further away than they actually are, and it's soon time to turn.

Maybe every day you spend by the coast has a moment like this, when the weather impinges for good or ill. That sudden emptying of silence that thunder brings. The sun marching from behind a cloud. The mist that wants to get in your pocket. And now, here, the wind. We turn and the breeze rearranges the day, and my hair. I feel an even deeper shorts-regret. It's cold; it's late June and it shouldn't be cold. We haven't lived through lockdowns, through those times when the grandchildren couldn't come in the house and so we had to do those drive-bys where we spoke through car windows and they gave me pictures and I gave them presents and I went back in the house and, as often as not, wept, to wander on a cold beach. In an unfair world, this seems pretty unfair. We should at least be warm, I say to myself; or maybe I say it aloud because my wife says 'You what?' and her words and mine are torn from our mouths and hurled down the coast towards Amble.

We walk into the wind like trainee mime artists. Sand animals appear and disappear, swirling and dancing. The clouds seem almost too heavy for the sky. 'I bet you're glad you put your shorts on' my wife says and I raise a sarcastic thumb. The tide is definitely coming in, bringing the wind with it, or vice versa. Occasionally the wind gets so strong that I'm reminded of that bit in *The Wizard of Oz* where Dorothy's house spins like a comedy bow tie. I half expect to see that bloke in the bathtub whirl by. My legs wish I'd put my trousers on.

As suddenly as it started, the wind stops. My hair rattles with sand-dandruff. A kite collapses. I don't have to raise my voice any more and I say 'That was cold, wasn't it?' My wife nods. We carry on walking, relieved that we don't have to lean into anything now. We talk about the café we are going to visit, about the possibilities of scones.

From out of nowhere the wind begins again. I find myself shivering. I put my mask on to protect my face. Come on, let's find a café where they sell scones and they don't sell gales.

THE SNAKE IN THE BED

My mother and my dad and I had put our suitcases down in the family room in the guest house in the small coastal town. The furniture was chocolate brown and heavy. The wardrobe gave me nightmares that week as I imagined all kinds of long-legged nastinesses dragging me in, accompanied by the sound of laughter.

There was a fold-up bed for me in the corner near a vast chest of drawers; I opened one of the drawers and there was a sock in it, and a set of playing cards. 'We should report that sock' my dad said, half joking because he was on holiday and out of office-mode. There was a TV with a screen as big as a tabloid newspaper and there was a gleaming white sink. I was eleven and I was on the verge of bodily changes that meant that my voice was breaking and a single dark piano wire of hair had started growing on my chest. I had a moustache that seemed to have been crocheted from limp wool and if I saw the corsets in my mother's Grattan catalogue I felt a prickling of sweat. Funny how the catalogue always seemed to fall open at that page.

Because my body was pummelling me on to the runway of adulthood, I was sulking most of the time and I found my parents to be the most embarrassing human beings in the world. Sometimes the old me would surface, gasping for air, and I would laugh at my dad's gags, but most of the time, I'm very sorry to say, I was spiky and abrasive. The gulls outside the room took the mickey out of me relentlessly and I don't blame them.

I was reading (please don't judge me) *The Grapes of Wrath* by John Steinbeck, having seen the film on a Saturday afternoon on TV. To be honest, I found it hard going and I confess that by the middle of the week I would abandon it and go back to Biggles and indeed spend a couple of book tokens on new Biggles books at the WH Smith in town, but for now, stubborn as a glacier, I was reading (performatively, if I'd known what the word meant at the time) *The Grapes of Wrath*, my brow furrowed so dramatically that it hurt. We were full of fish and chips and so we had an early night, mine punctuated by vivid dream-dioramas of Tom Joad being dragged into the wardrobe in the room by tall women in stockings and suspenders. The gulls screeched me awake at the break of dawn and I read the book under the covers.

We went down for breakfast and we were served by a girl in late teenage in one of those uniforms they used to wear in Lyons' Corner Houses and of course I thought she was the most beautiful person I'd ever seen. The white pinny over the black pinny. The black tights that of course, given my wardrobe dreams, I hoped were stockings. The gulls wheeled outside like animations. We all had a full English breakfast and I tried to eat the bacon in a way that showed I was a sophisticated man of the world. Well, boy of the world. She smiled at us but I was convinced that she was smiling at me. I smiled back but this was a mistake because I was just lifting a forkful of fried egg towards my pre-teen mouth and the effort of the smile was so gargantuan that I spilled yolk down the stripy polo shirt my mam had bought for the holiday, along with four more like it, from Smith's of West Melton. The yolk spread all over the canvas of the shirt, adding explosions and indoor fireworks to the stripes. My face went puce with embarrassment and I fought back tears. The waitress smiled but didn't laugh, which I saw as a good sign that we might one day meet up and get married after all.

My mother made my embarrassment even worse by grabbing the serviette and wiping my shirt, spreading the egg further and wider. We stood up and went back to the room, the breakfasts half-eaten; still, there was plenty on my clothes to fill us up later. The waitress smiled again as we left the room and my heart leaped like a goalkeeper saving a tricky free kick. Later, just before we went out, she knocked on our door; it turned out she was also a cleaner and now she was wearing a smock. There was (I'm not lying) a connection between us, and I saw her glance admiringly at *The Grapes of Wrath* on the bed, the Tufty Club bookmark sticking out like a tongue.

There was a joke shop in this small coastal town and I was allowed to go into it and spend some pocket money, the bit of pocket money I'd got left from buying books and comics. I considered a false moustache and some fake dog poo; I toyed with the idea of some soap that made you dirty; but eventually I settled on a realistic-looking plastic snake because I had an idea. An idea that Sigmund Freud could have written a book about.

My plan was to hide the plastic snake under the pillow with the head sticking out and then when the waitress who was also the cleaner saw it she'd scream but then laugh affectionately. I put the snake in my pocket and we went for a walk along the seafront. I smiled to myself; I hoped that the smile might look somehow seductive to passers-by although I guess that in reality it looked like a crack on a side plate.

Then I saw the young woman from the guest house walking in front of us; she wasn't alone. She was walking hand in hand with a lad who was obviously her boyfriend. He was, it seemed to me, the fattest and ugliest man I'd ever seen. 'There's the wee lassie from the guest house with her sweetheart,' said my dad. 'Don't worry, I won't tell her about your snake.'

What was that sound? Ah yes, the ground opening up and swallowing me whole. Like a mole. A mole with a chest hair. And a young boy choking back a sob.

THE OAR

Sometimes I picture myself in certain coastal situations: I'm on a bike (even though I can't ride a bike) riding along a clifftop path in a breeze with my scarf trailing behind me like steam from a train. I'm on a beach eating a sandwich and my mam and dad, long gone for many years, slip up quietly behind me. They are still young and full of the joys of life and love and we sit together eating and chatting. I am on a rowing boat on a still calm lake just by the sea; my wife and family are with me and we are laughing and somehow, in indefinable ways, I am The Best Dad Ever.

Well, the first two haven't happened and probably never will, although I live in hope, but the third one has. Mind you, the fact that in these domestic parts we refer to it as The Rowing Boat Incident might give you a hint that I wasn't in receipt of a Best Dad Ever badge that day. It was, as I recall, a cool day. Rain was forecast but not until later.

We'd been on the sands and we'd had an ice cream and now we decided that it would be good to go for a row around the boating lake. There was no breeze and there seemed to be no other hazards as far as we could see. I may have made an error there because in one sense, perhaps the most important sense, *I* was the hazard.

We got in the boat and it shifted alarmingly like a bouncy castle at a stag do. We all sat down and the ticket man handed me the oars. They were huge and weighty and it took me ages to get them into the rowlocks, a word I always enjoyed saying, mainly because I didn't have to use them practically. Now, I wasn't so sure. My smile was painted on and the paint began to dry.

Once my wife and kids had got settled and the boat had stopped dancing, the man pushed us away from the edge and we were afloat on the mirror-like water. I began to row and my shoulders pressed a button marked ACHE.

One of the kids shifted a little and the boat seemed to Titanic about a bit and I said in a 'soppy-stern' voice (to quote Philip Larkin) 'Please stop doing that. Please stop doing that now.' The kids and my wife sat like books on a shelf as we went further out towards the lake's centre. It was really shallow and you could see the bottom but I still began to feel a trickle of sweat down my back when my eldest daughter began to trail her hand through the water. I did my best to hide my anxiety from my family and, somehow, from the boat itself. It didn't work.

Another family approached in a different boat, laughing like an audience at the recording of a successful sitcom. I felt a sharp scratch of jealousy; their lives seemed uncomplicated and confident. They glided through the water like a merfamily. I redoubled my rowing efforts and my shoulders ached even more. Somehow, despite my efforts, we were drifting towards the edge of the lake as though we were the last drop of soup and the lake was a plate. My wife pointed out (unnecessarily in my view) that the edge was approaching. We bumped into it. The kids laughed and my pride took a tumble.

I pushed us away from the edge with the oar and we drifted into the lake again. I quite liked the drifting; it felt meditative and zen. It was as though I was floating above the floating. I could have been a character in a folk tale or a parable: The Man Who Floated Nowhere.

The kids were getting restive. My wife looked at her watch as a coded message to me to do something. I was secretly hoping that time was almost up and we would be called back imminently but that wasn't the case.

I took up my oars and began to row. Ah, maybe my hands had grown sweaty during the becalmed interregnum; perhaps I had unthinkingly dabbled the handle in the water and they had become slippery; perhaps fate and gravity were up for a laugh. Anyway, I dropped one of the oars and it floated away, half submerged, crocodile-style. My passengers (this is how I thought of them, as though I was the captain) looked on in horror with silent Munch *Scream* faces as the boat began to spin. It was only a saucer-deep lake in North-East Lincolnshire but it felt suddenly unpredictable. The oar continued to float away tauntingly. I tried to row towards it but seasoned canoeists will tell you that's a difficult operation with only one oar. We began to spin like a slowing globe on a bedroom windowsill. I rowed with one hand and one oar.

The family from before passed, still laughing, still packed with a kind of uncomplicated glee. I shouted 'Excuse me, could you just pass me my oar?'. They carried on laughing and rowed by, the dad's muscles gleaming, the mother looking at him adoringly, the kids stage-school burnished. The oar made its stately way towards the edge, the edge that I'd bumped into before.

Ah, 'before'; that time when everything was all right and I had two oars and a sense of purpose. Now I had one oar and a sense of futility.

Maybe I'm still there. Perhaps I never got off the lake. Maybe some kind souls in sou'westers rescued the family and they left me there for punishment. Been there for decades; become a tourist attraction like an exhibit in a freak show. Send sandwiches please, and a copy of *Moby-Dick* or *Mutiny on the Bounty*.

THE CURRENCY

My dad was a Scotsman, which meant that whenever Mr Coward the milkman came on a Friday for his money, his tall body silhouetted in the glass of our back door, he would always give my dad any Scottish pound notes and fivers he had in his change because, as he said, 'It'll make you feel at home', and my dad would sigh and swap the Bank of Scotland notes for Bank of England ones. In Mr Coward's head my dad would gaze at the money while listening to Andy Stewart and eating shortbread.

I was fascinated by the strange and exotic cash he handed over and I was even more intrigued when Mr Coward, warming to the task he'd devised on freezing early mornings on his humming float, started giving me coins from different parts of the country: shillings from Jersey and pennies from the Isle of Man, clinking in my pocket like little metal maps of possibilities. I read in my weekly *Treasure* magazine, a kind of improving journal for curious children, that they used to have cardboard currency on the Isle of Man and a footnote to the piece said that 'not much of the currency survives today', which as a child I found an almost impossibly magical statement; I couldn't articulate why but now I realise it was something to do with the properties of deep time versus the fragility of material things. They didn't put that in *Treasure*.

If they could have cardboard currency on the Isle of Man, I reasoned, then I could make some cardboard cash of my own and spend it. It was, I told myself, a simple but beautiful idea.

We were off on holiday to Llandudno later that week and that was where the Summer of the Cardboard Coins began. And ended, I guess, but I'm more interested in beginnings. I had the idea that I would make some cardboard money from old Frosties packets and try and spend it in the shops on the seafront and in my head if I got asked about the bendy pennies I would say that the money was legal tender in Yorkshire and the coins would be so well made that the gullible assistants would be taken in and I would somehow have got something over on somebody somewhere which is all a ten-year-old boy who read the *Beano* and *The Beezer* ever wanted to do.

It was fairly simple to make the coins; I simply traced round some half-crowns on the cardboard and cut them out. Imagine my tongue stuck out; imagine my brow furrowed like a ploughed field. Imagine the discarded cardboard when I got it wrong. Imagine the tears and tantrums when I discovered that we had no more empty cereal packets and my mother had to decant cereal into plastic tubs so that I had more cardboard. I decided to use half-crowns as templates partly because they were big enough to work with and also because they always looked unwieldy and otherworldly and because of that they might pass in a corner shop as legitimate currency.

I spent a while devising a name for the money; I didn't want to call them pounds shillings and pence because that seemed frankly dull and Mrs Stansfield said I was a clever boy who was good at making up stories so I should be able to make up backstories for loose change. In the end I settled on Salt. I was gazing around the room trying to think of a name and I'd rejected settee, windowframe and goldfish. My mother was pouring Cerebos salt into a salt pot and the name seemed to fit my jagged circles.

I could have called the money Cerebos but I was embarrassed because I didn't know how to pronounce it and even as a ten-year-old I intuited that if you made new money you should be able to talk about it with confidence.

Fast-forward now to Llandudno. Take a panning shot along a parade of shops and settle on a branch of WH Smith that I'm about to enter with my cardboard money in my purse. I'm nervous and excited. I feel like I'm about to perform a criminal act. With cardboard.

I go to the endless array of comics and I pick up a *Dandy*. It seems that Korky the Cat and I are in cahoots because this is the kind of stunt he would come up with. Somehow, because this is all happening in the endlessly music hall space of the seaside it won't matter in the least that I'm buying something with buckshee dosh because here, littorally, anything goes.

I walk to the counter. A man who looks a bit like he wishes he was elsewhere takes my *Dandy* and looks at it. This is pre-history so of course he didn't scan it because a barcode in those far-off days was a request not to wear trainers or to put on a tie. He looks at the price and rings it up on an ancient till. He tells me the price and I pretend I'm searching in my purse for the money. The cardboard feels very malleable, like old lard.

My mother and dad are at the other end of the shop; he is going to buy a *Trout & Salmon* magazine and she is trying to decide between *Woman's Own* and *Woman*. I give the bloke two Cardboard Coins and say 'I'm sorry I've nothing smaller. Can you change a Salt?' and even as I say the words I know that this whole endeavour will be a seaside failure and not even a glorious seaside failure. It will be like the moment when my mate Mark tried to get into a Pink Floyd concert at Sheffield City Hall with a KitKat wrapper on which he'd written the words PINK FLOYD TICKET in red felt-tip. The man holds up the cardboard coins. He waves them at a man in a suit who I take to be the manager.

All my lines about the history of cardboard coinage slip from my head. I need a prompt but one isn't forthcoming.

I'll tell you what I am at this moment: I am a character in a cartoon. I am in the *Dandy*. I've tried one jape too many. The besuited manager glides across the floor. I hope my mother decides which magazine she's buying soon. Very soon.

THE HUNSTANTON FRISBEE
INCIDENT

Here he is, Jolly Old Ian McMillan, so jolly that he was once called 'relentlessly jolly' by the *Guardian* and so jolly about being called 'relentlessly jolly' by the *Guardian* that he put the quote on the business cards he had printed. He's jolly because he's on his holidays with his young family at the North Norfolk resort of Hunstanton. The sun is a beach ball; the sky is a summer dress.

The McMillan family have been to the slot machines and watched 2p pieces obeying or not obeying the laws of gravity. They've attempted to grab cuddly toys from a pile of cuddly toys with the aid of a grabber. They've bought souvenir rock for relatives and schoolfriends. There's a mist of sadness behind the jollity because this is the last day of the holiday when everything seems at once very close and really far away; here are times that will never come again, here are moments that will only ever exist as photographs or stories. And all the stories will soon be in the past imperfect tense.

For now, though, the jollity is winning out and Jolly Old Ian McMillan is being jollier than ever in an attempt to ward off the melancholy that might truly descend when the cottage has to be cleaned up later. Ian McMillan decides to do a daft thing; he decides to run along the beach going Whooooooo. The kids laugh and Ian's wife laughs kindly at the always eager-to-please clown she married all those years ago.

The man in the picture, the man in the Ian mask, is not built for running along the beach; these days he has slimmed down quite a lot but at the time we're calling Hunstanton Time he was a big unit. He took up quite a bit of North Norfolk. He is running because he feels it is his parental duty to be jolly and happy and make other people happy and jolly and so he runs to make people happy. A bit like Alf Tupper did.

The sun is still a beach ball; the sky is still a summer dress. At the other end of the beach there's another family. The McMillans have seen them around and the kids are the same age and the parents seem to be around the same age as McMillan and Wife, to quote the name of an old American TV show that used to tauntingly follow Jolly Ian around at school. 'Where's yer wife? Hey, it's McMillan and…'

The man of the family is not like Jolly I. He is tall and often shirtless and the shirtlessness shows off his muscles. He looks like a relief map of himself. During the week he has nodded at Ian with a nod that combines pity with a gleaming cheerfulness that he is not shaped like Jolly I. In his head Ian calls this gent The Muscle Man. Is Ian jealous? No, he is content to be jolly. Oh, come on; is Ian jealous of the man's torso and legs and arms? Well, he's a combination of jealous and jolly. He's Jealolly, which looks on the page a bit like a representation in language of the way Ian McJolly's man-breasts shiver and shake as he walks. Or in this case as he runs down the beach.

The Muscle Man is about to throw a Frisbee in such a way that his tattoos will be like animations. Of course he is about to throw a Frisbee. The sea is a still mirror and a gull whirls like a sixteenth-century automaton and TMM is going to chuck a Frisbee-shaped hole into this timeless diorama. Some people are fans of Frisbees and see them as harmless mid-Atlantic fun but Ian

McJolly isn't one of these. You can call him a miserable bugger if you like but there's something performative and showy-off about Frisbees that rubs Ian's library-loving heart up the wrong way. For I McJ, the Frisbee is the equivalent of The Muscle Man's pectoral mountains.

The children are still laughing though as their daft dad runs; maybe it is better to be a daft dad at the seaside than an oiled Adonis of a father. Discuss: or rather don't, because the Frisbee is about to reach warp speed. It's the last day of the holiday and tomorrow will be the long slow car trip home and the picnic in the lay-by and the silence that slowly spills over into a badly rehearsed fractiousness.

Jolly Ian is now seriously out of breath and he is wheezing huge creaking wheezes. His face is a beef tomato. He sweats fire buckets.

The Frisbee floats towards him and in certain lights it could be a spaceship containing intelligent multicellular and vortex-brained beings that have come to explore Hunstanton with a view to setting up coastal fish farms. Ian McMillan's run has slowed to a walk, then an amble, then a stumble, then something that is almost stasis. The Frisbee is getting closer. One of the kids, the youngest one, the boy who will become a prize-winning poet, shouts 'Dad!' Muscle Man shouts 'Watch it mate!' and even his voice is so strong it has a six-pack and could lift saloon cars.

Jolly, jolly Ian McMillan couldn't move out of the way of the Frisbee even if he wanted to. Above him the sky darkens. There's a whisper of something whizzing through the air. Almost at the last moment Ian McJ looks up and then wishes he hadn't looked anywhere as the Frisbee clonks him on the bonce.

Ian leans over and begins to sway palm-in-a-breezishly. He is partly acting, it's true, but the Frisbee collision hurt quite a bit. His swaying becomes more exaggerated until he is The Leaning

Tower of Ian. The kids don't know whether to laugh or cry. The Muscle Man's Mouth is a big muscular O. Ian's wife looks worried.

Only Ian knows if he's really hurt. It's the last day of the holidays. He decides to keep them guessing. It'll be something to talk about on the journey home.

COAST AS A SERIES OF NOVELTY CRUET SETS

That cruet set at the cottage in Beadnell in the shape of two stumpy lighthouses. A cruet set, one with MY SAND LIFE, one with MY PEBBLE LIFE on, in a sandy/pebbly font. Which is salt and which is pepper? You decide. Those two rusting forts in the Humber Estuary off Cleethorpes; imagine the wide flat water as a wide flat tablecloth and the two forts as a salt pot and a pepper pot. In an odd way this humanises them, makes them less rusty and more welcoming. Which is salt and which is pepper? You decide.

Those two gulls on the back of that bench by the sea, the bench that often has a little posy of flowers by it, in memory of someone who loved that view of that particular tranche of changing light. One could be a salt gull and one could be a pepper gull. Slowly, because a pair of (novelty cruet set) yappy dogs are approaching, they wheel into the sky in a way that no cruet sets have ever done unless they were chucked comedically in a seaside hotel breakfast room row. ('Look out! It'll be the toast rack next, lad!') Unless of course they were automatons, those mechanical precursors of robots that amazed people in cathedrals. An automaton gull novelty cruet set; imagine those for sale in a gift shop in a Cornish seaside town. How could you ever resist them? Imagine them cranking up from the table and creakingly flapping around the room, reminding you of that holiday, those endless days.

Old couple in huddle mode novelty cruet set in a shelter on a drizzly day as the North Sea appears to look bigger and wetter and less welcoming than it actually is. He is, valiantly, trying to read a newspaper. He's from that generation that buys a tabloid then folds it into the size of a pocket square. She is gazing into space, thinking of when they were young and he could fold the paper so tightly that it could never be unfolded. If they're a novelty cruet set, then the eternal question is beckoning: who's the salt, who's the pepper?

Ah, to check that out you'd have to walk past the shelter and then, on some pretext, look at the tops of their heads. Three holes in the top of his flat cap? One hole in the top of her headscarf? Vice versa? That'll tell you.

He's folded the paper to the Quick Crossword, and as he often says in moments of holiday exasperation, 'If that's a quick crossword then I'm Freddie and the Dreamers', a saying that feels neither sage nor wise. He reads the clues aloud to his unimpressed wife and today they all seem to be coast-related. He says: 'Cliffs crumbling away question mark: Summat R summat S summat summat summat.' 'Erosion' his wife says, her words hanging in the damp air. He writes it down. He says 'Temporary beach structure: Summat summat summat summat summat summat summat summat summat E.' 'Sandcastle' she says. 'I'd have got to it after a bit' he says. Close relatives of the novelty cruet set are the snow globe and the funny but heart-warming jigsaw and the oddly shaped and brightly coloured fridge magnet. Imagine these two in a snow globe, maybe on a winter break, shivering in this shelter. Imagine these two on a funny but heart-warming jigsaw. Yes, they'd end up in a charity shop, but we all will. Imagine them as a pair of fridge magnets like cartoon versions of themselves magnetised to a white metal door in some kind of eternal torment because they can smell the contents but never get to taste them. All these variations are fine but in my mind the novelty cruet set is best.

Summer sun and summer moon as novelty cruet set. Don't look too closely at the sun of course; maybe look at its reflection in a bucket of water and you'll wonder why nobody thought of this before. That late evening you and her walked alone on the quiet promenade, with the full moon like a mystical monocle. You gaze at the sky and wonder why nobody had the cruet set idea before. The way the sun defined your holiday; the search for it, the way you tried to use the power of your will to force it out from behind the clouds. The way the sun dictated how much sun cream you put on and how big your sun hat was. The way the sun whispered to you: 'Go on, take your shirt off, nobody will ever notice that scribble of hair around your belly button' and you believed the sun and you did and they did. The way the moon seemed to be your friend, just lighting the sky for the two of you. The way the moon seemed to be telling you that you would be young forever and that, year after year, like a couple in a romcom, you would return to this spot and walk holding hands under the full moon and the waves would be crashing just for you. And then one day in a charity shop you'd see the novelty sun and moon cruet set that we have together somehow dreamed into being and you'd buy it and take it home and when you had fish and chips you'd pretend you were at the seaside and the salt and pepper would cascade on to the chips in a way that made you think of sand.

Two caravans as a novelty cruet set, and two tents. Two sticks of rock as a novelty cruet set, and two giant humbugs. Two postcards home rendered in ceramic and turned into a novelty cruet set. Weather pepper, wish you were salt.

The tide comes in and the tide goes out; stand there, both of you, and imagine what it would be like if you stood there forever. Like a novelty cruet set might.

YOUNG MAN WITH A NOTEBOOK

A passing van, maybe a postal worker's van rattling along the island's skinny roads, would have noticed a boy with an architecture of hair carefully closing the door of a big double-fronted house that operated as a B&B. There was a big NO VACANCIES sign in the window, and the boy coming out of the door was part of the NO VACANCIES. His mam and dad slept, indeed snored, upstairs. It was early in the morning and the day's paint was still wet.

A hawk circling like an LP on a turntable would see the boy walk across the road and pause at the other side, looking around and trying to take everything in. The sea is a mirror of the blue sky, already bright at this early hour because it is June and the days are almost too long to fit the calendar. The hawk would have noticed that the boy is carrying a notebook. If the hawk was a fan of poetry (and who knows, it may be. They are the subject of many.), it may have concluded that the boy looked a little bit from above like the young Dylan Thomas and this would have pleased the boy very much because the boy wants nothing more than to be a poet and he has been soaking in Dylan Thomas since he discovered his poems in Darfield Library one rainy Friday evening just before Mrs Dove said 'Seven o'clock please' and I prepared to go.

Yes, the boy is me. I am on holiday with my parents on the Isle of Skye. It's my first time on this transcendent and singing rock and I am fourteen years old and the cauldron of adolescence is bubbling and smoking and I want so desperately to be a poet that I am taking every opportunity to slip away from my mother and dad who, as far as I'm concerned, live on a planet inhabited by war memories and fly-tying, to write poems that are so tortured I'm surprised their bones don't shatter and their muscles shred.

A gull on a fence near the footpath to the sea that we wandered down last night sees me take out my notebook and begin to write about it, trying to distil its feathery essence into a learner poet's overheated lines. God bless all learner poets, I say, with L plates on their stanzas. They are learning the scales of language.

I write, in handwriting so bruised and turbulent that only I can read it *I am the gull with wings so clipped by boredom that I cannot fly. If I die I will just be a mountain of feathers pushed away by the wind.*

Not bad. I'll keep that and work on it later then maybe send it to a poetry magazine like *Outposts* or *Pink Peace*. The gull flaps away and is absorbed into the distance. I walk along the pebbly beach towards the shore. The urge to be a poet is stronger in me than the urge to write poems. In my head I am receiving an award for my first collection, entitled The Uig Poems, Uig being a place name on Skye that rings in my head. In my head a sequence about Skye will form the centrepiece of the as-yet-unwritten volume. Suddenly, as though I am the first person to think of it, I write *Skye sky* in the notebook, swiftly followed by *sea see*. Maybe I'll call the book *Skye Sky*. I see it in a bookshop. I see somebody buying it in a bookshop.

I walk further and I write *the seen sea meets the Skye sky.* I am absurdly pleased. Far ahead of me a couple are walking, hand in hand. Even though I can't see him properly I'm sure that he is ugly and even though I can't see her properly I'm sure she is beautiful and mysterious. Maybe, in my teenage head, she is as beautiful and mysterious as Emma Peel in *The Avengers.* They stand looking out to sea; the waves are making splashing noises and gulls are whirling. I bend and pick up a pebble and pocket it because I want it to remind me forever of this moment on this beach with my notebook and that couple. I might even have the pebble for the front cover of The Uig Poems. I might send a copy to Diana Rigg when it comes out.

Overhead, the sky is getting changed, putting on darker clothes. The breeze is revving up. I look at my watch: ages till breakfast. I walk towards the couple; it's not that I want to talk to them. God forbid that I should want to talk to them. I'm fourteen and I don't want to talk to anybody. I just want to write about them, to put them in my sequence.

Now they are standing facing each other. Her hair is blowing in the wind, as is his because this is the very early 1970s and everybody, even newsreaders and police chiefs, has got long hair. *Wind like seaweed in the air's sea* I write in my book and although that's not quite right I can work on it later in the B&B's residents' lounge as my mother and dad watch *Bonanza* on a black-and-white TV that frays at the edges of the picture and the landlady brings in tea on a tray.

I stop and watch in wonder and a kind of growing horror as the couple stand even closer and he puts his hand on her bum. I don't know where to look/I know exactly where to look. They kiss and I am about to spontaneously combust. I am angry that I am not that man. I am angry that I am a lad with a notebook. I am angry with the sea; I am so angry with the sea. It can just hang around being the sea.

The couple stop kissing for a moment and a few drops of rain are parachuted from the sky. A storm is coming. The young woman turns and sees me and waves. She waves! Maybe she'll buy my book once I've written it and she'll recognise herself in it.

The rain is pouring down. There's a distant shout of thunder. The couple and I run from the beach but we run in separate directions because they are local and I am not. My notebook is getting wet and I push it under my shirt to keep the words dry. I am almost at the B&B. I am almost there. They were kissing. He had his hand on her bum.

TOWELS AND TRUNKS

On this family holiday one thing is occupying me above all others, above my anxiety about finding new Biggles books in the WH Smith I visited last year in the same seaside resort, above my hope that my dad won't snore with a sound like a giant cement mixer in a submarine. I am worried about getting changed into my trunks to go for a paddle. I am just about to ascend the foothills of adolescence and I am becoming aware of my body and I see it as a butter sculpture created by a first-timer at a butter sculpture evening class in a dusty community centre.

As my mother explains it, there are two trunk-options: I can put my trunks on in the guest-house room before we go down to the beach or I can put them on under a towel when we get to the beach. My mother was always a great explainer, turning everything into a story you could learn from. As she pointed out, there were advantages and disadvantages to each approach: Trunks On In The Room was probably easier, but it meant that you had to walk back with wet trunks on. Trunks On On The Beach meant that you were always at the mercy of a sea breeze lifting the towel Marilyn Monroe style just as you were pantless and just as the Chester WI annual trip was trooping by discussing jam. 'We might need bigger jars' one of them might be heard to say. My dad, who had faced high seas and explosions and evenings carrying naked sailors back to the ship from overcrowded brothels, said 'Just take your trousers off and put your trunks on. Nobody will notice.' I went redder than a matador's cape and burrowed into a self-indulgent sulk. In the end, the possible exposure of flesh won out over the damp stroll back and I decided to change into my trunks on the beach.

The day was overcast and so we reasoned that the beach might not be too busy and that people might be scattered across the shore like pieces in a chess endgame or a crowd at a reserve match. We were wrong; the beach looked like Woodstock. There was hardly a spare inch of sand. We almost turned back but luckily a large family vacated a spot just as we arrived; it's decades ago but I can still remember the disgruntled dad saying, in the high-pitched siren voice of the entitled posh, 'You broke the cup and it's on your shoulders.' The phrase has haunted me for so long that I almost called one of my collections of poetry after it to exorcise the ghost.

We settled into their vacated space. My dad spread a tartan rug on the sand; from a distance it would have looked like a melted Highland Chieftain. Our picnic basket went on top, and my dad opened the flask and poured tea for him and my mother. He poured it triumphantly, celebrating the parking place we'd acquired. The sun came out to join in the fun. In the next space a bored boy who could almost have been me defiantly read *The Beezer* as his dad encouraged him to dig sandcastles with his little sister. He was wearing trunks and folds of fat almost rendered them invisible. He looked like I would if I had trunks on, I reasoned to myself. I wished I'd brought a Biggles book with me.

My dad said 'Let's go for a paddle. Get your trunks on!' I almost began a second sulk-fest but then my mother said 'Come on, I'll hold the towel round' and I felt such a tidal wave of love for her that I decided I'd put them on.

They were fished out of the bag. They were a kind of duck-egg blue if the ducks had survived a nuclear holocaust and become radioactive. I felt the boy with *The Beezer's* eyes on me. Over the years, as a poet and performer, I've come to enjoy having people look at me; I've become a show-off and someone who is very comfortable being the centre of attention. Indeed, my wife will say that I crave attention, which is probably true. The younger me didn't, though. The younger me avoided mirrors and would have enjoyed living on an uninhabited island thereby making it no longer an uninhabited island.

My mother held the towel up. I stood behind it and it was as though I was behind the curtains at a theatre and I was about to come out for my big number in a musical. I would have been wearing a certain outfit in the first act and I would have got changed into something spectacular in the interval. I was nervous. I took my trousers off. My mother held the towel. My dad said, 'Hurry up lad, your mum's arms will be getting tired.' I don't want to suggest that my dad was an impatient man; far from it. He just, in his Royal Navy way, wanted to get the job done efficiently while the sea was looking.

I picked up the trunks my trousers were round my ankles I kicked off the trousers and held my trunks in one hand and pulled my pants down with the other and I pulled hard and they began to slide and I held the trunks and my mam held the towel and the sound of the people on the beach seemed very far away and my pants were off and I was exposed to the world except I wasn't I was behind the all-encompassing towel in the comfortable room of the towel and a breeze blew round my nether areas from somewhere and I threw the pants down and I hopped into one leg of the trunks and my mam pretended to drop the towel and laughed but I didn't laugh and then I hopped some more and pulled the trunks up and pulled them up and they were on and she dropped the towel.

'Let's go paddling' my dad said. My mother folded up the towel and somehow my nakedness and a moment of growing up were folded away inside it.

TIDE OUT

My dad was a keen but sporadic amateur photographer; he took his cue from my aforementioned Uncle Charlie, who was a dedicated and not-sporadic amateur photographer and who was always encouraging my dad to take more photographs wherever he went. 'Always have the camera ready, Jack,' he would say, calling my dad Jack even though his name was John.

How do you end a book like this? How do I end this particular book that was born out of a desire to follow myself around the coast and has ended up being a following of my mind and memories around the coast, sometimes with the tide of detail in and sometimes with the tide of detail so far out that you can see the other side. The side with no details, just broad brushstrokes the colour of sand.

The idea for this book came in the before times, the pre-lockdown utopia when all we had to worry about was austerity and climate catastrophe. It continued with me climbing the stairs to the spare bedroom and fishing in my head for coast stories. Somehow by doing this I invented, or rather reinvented the coast for myself. The coast I wrote about was a solipsistic one, revolving around me and my memories. If the tide came in or went out it only did so because I was there. Somehow, as I wrote the book in one-thousand-word chunks, it became about making a life available for myth. It felt odd but satisfying as the country and the world locked down and opened up and locked down and opened up. We all have our own coasts, of course. We are, despite what the poem says, islands. This has been a map of mine.

One evening at Uncle Charlie's in the mid-1960s, the light was fading and Auntie was putting the kettle on. It was almost time to look at the slides, the colour (often technicolour) photographs that Uncle Charlie had taken. He'd got the projector out ready and now he switched it on; it was like someone had switched on a moon rocket. The noise was deafening and I was surprised Mrs Beck next door, dozing after her early shift on the Yorkshire Traction buses, didn't bang on the wall with her ticket machine. After a while it settled down to a low hum; above it, dust motes danced in the heat. Auntie turned the lights off and the projector defined a screen on the wall. My heart sank a little, but only a little, when Uncle Charlie fished out loads of boxes of slides. I might not get back home in time for *Voyage to the Bottom of the Sea*.

There we were on the beach in hand-knitted cardigans because there was a sneaky edge to the wind. There I was eating a pork pie. There was my dad asleep on a deckchair. There was my mam looking glamorous as she always did, even when serving plates of sandwiches in a tight caravan. There's my brother in a fantastic pork-pie hat, the hat he called his Robin Hood Hat. Here are our memories of a recent holiday projected on a wall. It's as though we're at Wombwell Plaza and we're being shown on the big screen. It's as though our lives are important.

The door opens and we can hear Little Charlie coming in; he's Uncle Charlie's son and he's also called Charlie so we call him Little Charlie. He's been on days at the pit and it sounds like he's called at the club on his way home. There's an impression of stumbling, of being on a boat in a rocking sea. He opens the door and sashays across the room, walking straight into the blinding light of the projector. I am projected on to his face and his shirt. It is as though for a moment he is on holiday with us. Maybe that could be one place to think about ending the book; someone caught in the light, held in someone else's narrative.

UP THE PATH

It's July 2021 and the Covid unlocking continues; some of the poetry and music gigs that me and my mate Luke Carver Goss do, having been postponed in 2020, are reappearing and we're playing at the lovely Kirkgate Centre in Cockermouth and I have a plan. I have a Coast-based plan that's going to form some kind of ringing, symphonic climax to this book. After all the interior journeys there will be an exterior journey. A sea breeze will ruffle my hair like an affectionate auntie might. There may be a view of a watery horizon; in my mind I will sip espresso at a bijou beachside café and pretend I'm in a contemporary novel or a Sundance film. I won't just be unshaven; I'll have stubble.

After the Cockermouth gig I will stay in somebody's spare room and the next morning I will catch the 7.08 bus to Workington and I will walk by the sea to remind myself that the sea is still there and I will make some kind of narrative, something that draws the whole story together. I've been to Workington before, but there is coast there and there is sea and there are clouds that float over the sea and that is good enough for me. Then I'll catch the train to Carlisle and slowly rattle home.

I excitedly tell the organisers of the gig about my plan and one of them comes up to me in the dressing room where I am supping tea. He is wearing a mask and so I stop supping tea and put my mask back on. He tells me, through fabric, that all the trains from Workington to Carlisle or, as he puts it, 'from Workington to anywhere' are cancelled the following day. My heart sinks; I had looked forward so much to this finale. I had, let's be frank, half-written some of the sentences and quarter-toned a few of the paragraphs. I could get a few buses, of course, but I wanted the indefinable romance of rail. I am crestfallen. Coastally crestfallen. I am so crestfallen that I drink some tea through my mask.

Then Luke stops cleaning his accordion and offers a solution. 'I'll drive you to Workington and we'll have a wander by the water,' he says, and suddenly the dressing room light seems stronger and brighter and my life seems to have more purpose.

Then it's time to do the gig and it goes like a dream to say neither of us have performed in public for more than a year and all through the two halves and the encore the coast beckons. The coast beckons, smiling.

I stay in the house of someone who has a railway in his garden and late into the night I watch engines trundle round between the roses as sheep bleat on the hills beyond the fence. There is a subtle cruelty to this because there are no real trains for me to gaze at in the morning. The tide has gone out on my first plan for tomorrow and the tide has come in on my second plan. The weather forecast isn't good but that doesn't bother me; the present is rubbing the past away and I'm here to make memories, not dredge them up. I ask my host about bijou cafés in Workington and he thinks hard and suggests a place that might, he thinks, still be open.

I sleep fitfully, dreaming of giant gulls carrying me away as though I am a chip.

Luke and I drive to Workington; the town is like New York in that it is built on a grid system and people are rushing along the grids like characters in a video game. I visit the Luckiest Lottery Shop In Cumbria, planning what I'm going to do with my millions. I'll let them change my life. Clouds build huge walls and so we decide to go to Slag Bank, a place that somebody at the gig the night before recommended to us. I like the way the two syllables are like the sound of boots on a path or shouts when you tread on something sharp. I like the way there is no room for romance in the univowelled words.

In the car park a man and his wife eat bacon sandwiches and drink steam from a flask. Dozens of dogs drag owners up the narrow path towards the top of the banks, which are literally piles of slag from old ironworks on a peninsula that juts out to the sea. We walk up the hill, past an iron crucifix that was erected by a local man, Peter Nelson, in 2014 in memory of his wife. There's something stark and unforgiving about it, like the landscape itself.

It's starting to rain. I had another plan that I didn't want to tell Luke about. I wanted him to take his piano accordion up to the top of the slag bank and he could improvise a piece that was part elegy for, part celebration of the sea that I'd been thinking about so much for the past year and a bit. The plangent sound of the accordion would carry a long way and maybe (in my head) the dog walkers and their dogs would form a circle around Luke as he played and one of the dogs would begin to howl and then they all would.

And Luke would begin to play more quietly and I would tell one of the stories that I'd been gathering for this book, and then I'd tell another. Occasionally Luke would play a little louder but then he would dip under my voice and provide what they call a bed in the world of broadcast audio.

Then a small coastal miracle would happen. Someone would step out of the circle and into the middle. They would start to tell us all, tell you all, about their sand life, their pebble life. The dogs would howl quietly in a kind of dogharmony. The rain would stop.

This didn't happen, of course. The rain got heavier. Luke and I stood at the top of the slag bank and I regretted that I was wearing a cheap suit. This didn't feel like a bijou café; the sea looked like the kind of tea you imagine got served in prison in the 1950s. We turned and wandered back to the car. I imagined this as a kind of ending; it isn't. I need to go back inside. Back inside myself.

MY SAND LIFE MY PEBBLE LIFE

My sand life, my pebble life.
This sand life, this pebble life.
This pebble life, this sand life.
My pebble life, my sand life.
My tide life, my sea life.
My shore life, my sand life.
This edge life, this coast life.
This lived life, this living life.
My only life, my held life.
This held life, this only life.
This remembered life, this life.
This life, this remembered life.
This masked life, this unmasked life.
My masked life, my unmasked life.
My cloud life, my rain life.
My sun life, my cloud life.
My rain life, my sun life.
This cloud life, this rain life.
My sand life, my pebble life.
My   life, my pebble life.
My sa   life, my   life.
My s   life, m   l
My   life